A Commentary on
JAMES

UNLOCKING THE NEW TESTAMENT

A Commentary on
JAMES

David Pawson

Anchor Recordings

First published in Great Britain in 2015 by
Anchor Recordings Ltd
72 The Street, Kennington, Ashford TN24 9HS

**For more of David Pawson's teaching,
including DVDs and CDs, go to
www.davidpawson.com**

**FOR FREE DOWNLOADS
www.davidpawson.org**

**For further information, email
info@davidpawsonministry.com**

ISBN 978-1-909886-72-8

Printed by Lightning Source

Contents

This book is based on a series of talks. Originating as it does from the spoken word, its style will be found by many readers to be somewhat different from my usual written style. It is hoped that this will not detract from the substance of the biblical teaching found here.

As always, I ask the reader to compare everything I say or write with what is written in the Bible and, if at any point a conflict is found, always to rely upon the clear teaching of scripture.

David Pawson

1
INTRODUCTION AND INSIGHT

Read James 1:1

A. WRITER – James, Lord's brother, in Jerusalem
    1. His story
        a. Life
        b. Death
    2. His strengths
        a. Scripture
        b. Prayer

B. READERS – Messianic Jews in Diaspora
    1. Their story
        a. A second scattering
        b. Voluntary
    2. Their weaknesses
        a. Wealth
        b. Gossip
        c. Divisions
        d. Assimilation

C. LETTER
    1. Form – general
        a. Name and address
        b. People or places?
    2. Style – typical
        a. Hebrew wisdom
        b. Greek diatribes?
    3. Content – ethical
        a. Deity
        b. Doctrine?

We have the name of the writer right at the beginning: James. If you are from Scotland, you will remember the Jacobite Rebellion in Scotland against the royal house of James. For, actually, James is only an English name and if you read this letter in Greek it says in v. 1 *Iacobus* which we might pronounce "Yakov", which is "Jacob". So this man was named after Abraham's grandson. Therefore we should not really call it the letter of James, we should call it the letter of Jacob. But for Anglophone readers I use "James".

The problem is that there are at least four (if not five) people in the New Testament called James or Jacob. So one of the questions we have to ask right at the beginning is: which James was it? It may be that it was one of the last books in the New Testament to be included because they were not sure who had written it. Most people are sure that it was James the half-brother of Jesus. Mary, as you know, was a virgin until Jesus was born. Then she had other children: four sons, two daughters. We do not know the daughters' names but we know the four sons' names. One was called Jacob or James, and another was called Judas. But he did not like that name for obvious reasons, so he shortened it to Jude. We have two letters from those two half-brothers of Jesus in our New Testament.

The story of this man is very interesting. When he was living at home with Jesus in Nazareth, keeping the carpentry business going, he and his brothers were very sceptical of Jesus. Indeed, on one occasion the whole family came while he was preaching, to take him and shut him up at home. They were convinced he was schizophrenic. They did not use that word then of course. They said, "He is beside himself; he's two people and he's gone crazy on one side." So they intended to shut him away from the public. At that point Jesus said, "Who is my brother and who is my mother? Whoever does the will of my Father in heaven is my brother." That was a poke in the eye for Mary as well as his brothers.

They also teased him after he claimed to be the Messiah. Since the Messiah was expected at the Feast of Tabernacles they teased him when that feast came round and said, "Aren't you going to go up to the Feast of Tabernacles and show yourself?" He went up secretly after that, without their knowledge. But they were teasing him. All his life, up to his death, his brothers were against him, even mocking. James must have remembered that with embarrassment as he looked back on those days with shame. You can guess how he felt. In fact, he felt so bad when Jesus died on a cross that he stopped eating and said he would not eat food again and would starve to death. Fortunately, Jesus rose from the dead three days later and James had to end his fast. We know that Jesus, after he had risen from the dead, made a special appearance to James. It was after all the others – after he had appeared to the twelve and after he had appeared to five hundred at once. Then it says he appeared to James, the second last appearance. The last of course was to Paul (or Saul of Tarsus as he was then). So James had a special appearance in the resurrection. Presumably his brother Judas (not Iscariot) did as well, because they became what they called "slaves of Jesus Christ". They had completely changed their attitude toward their half-brother.

So after years of mocking and even disliking their half-brother, they changed at the resurrection and both became leading Christians. In fact, James became the chairman of the Jerusalem church and the chairman of the biggest council they held in those days. It is all in Acts 15. The issue was whether there would be two churches, one for Jewish believers and the other for Gentiles, or whether they could keep them together and have just "one new man in Christ Jesus". James was entrusted with the delicate and difficult task of keeping the church together and avoiding this first big split in those days. That would have lasted until today, had it happened. But James was a wise man. He was a loved man, and therefore he attracted a lot of nicknames.

His first nickname when he was at home was "James the Little". So we presume he was not as tall as his brothers. After he became the leader and accepted chairman of the Jerusalem church, and therefore the Jerusalem council, they called him by another nickname: "James the Just" or "James the fair". Later still they gave him another nickname, "James the bulwark" – the pillar of the church. He did have that honour. He was not one of the Twelve, nevertheless he was the most important believer in the first church in Jerusalem. He had already written to Gentiles in the whole dispersed area advising them about the Jews and telling them to observe the Jewish scruples – not because they were under the law but to keep fellowship, and therefore to observe kosher food, for example. That would keep the Gentiles and Jews together in the fellowships that were composed of both. So he was wise. That was another one of his nicknames: "James the wise" – the sort of man you can't do without, who can hold the church together when it is liable to split.

Of course the big issue then was: can Gentiles become Christians and believe in the Jewish Messiah without becoming Jews? Of course the sign of becoming a Jew was circumcision. That was the issue the council in Acts 15 was called to discuss. They appealed to two different things. They appealed to what the Spirit said and they appealed to what the scripture said. Where those two agree, that should settle it. It is a very simple approach to a church division. Peter appealed to what the Spirit was doing with a Gentile called Cornelius. James appealed to scripture: the book of Amos chapter 9, where God clearly wants to include Gentiles in his people, not as Jews but as Gentiles. So that is James, a just man who could hold Christians together when they were arguing, one who could be a peacemaker in the church.

That is a little about his life. But let us move on to his death, because we know from a Roman historian called Eusebius that it was a remarkable martyrdom. What happened was that there was a gap in Jerusalem between two Roman governors. The governor before whom Paul had been tried had now retired and gone and there was a two-month wait before his successor came from Rome. Therefore there was that little window of time when the Jews were not directly under a Roman governor. At that point the high priest virtually took over the governor's place, and his name was Annas. He had been high priest when Jesus himself had been tried. Now he had this problem: a growing church with thousands of people coming into it and hundreds of priests coming into it. He has got this little window of two months to get rid of the early church, and he took it by arresting James, the head of the church. He realised that the church was held together by this little wise man.

So they arrested him and ordered him, appropriately, to be thrown off the pinnacle of the temple. They must have remembered Jesus' temptation to throw himself off. So there is almost a mockery in this by Annas: let's see if angels stop you being hurt, we are going to throw you off the pinnacle of the temple. They did, and he crashed to the ground and must have broken many bones. But it didn't kill him. So Annas then gave the order for him to be stoned to death. The poor broken man, full of broken bones, is now being stoned – big, heavy rocks thrown at him. That didn't kill him either. In fact, his reaction to being thrown off the temple was to say, "Father, forgive them." His reaction to being stoned, which should have killed him, was to pray again for their forgiveness and to say, "I see the Son of Man seated on the throne of heaven." It was very like Stephen's martyrdom. Still the stoning didn't kill him, so finally a Jewish soldier took a club and smashed his skull in, and that is how he died. Christians took his body for burial and they discovered an amazing thing. When they stripped the body to wash it and wrap it up they discovered his knees were great large knobbly knees. So he became known as "James of knobbly knees". They were like the knees of a camel. Have you ever seen a camel's knees? Great lumps of hard flesh in the middle of their legs. We are told that he got his knees like that by endlessly praying on the stone floor of the temple that God would forgive the Jews for what they did to his Son. Isn't it ironic that he should be spending all that time praying for the people who put him to death?

So he was a man of prayer. There are four occasions in this little letter in which he gives us teaching on prayer, and each time he gives us the reason why some prayers are not answered. So if you have got a problem of unanswered prayer, read through James' letter and he will give you at least four reasons why the Lord is not listening to you. He was not only strong on the prayer side, but he was strong on the scripture side. Through this letter you will find that he was constantly appealing first to the Old Testament and to people in it like Abraham and *Rahav*, or Rahab as we call her, or Elijah. He was soaked in scripture. Now of course the New Testament had not then been written – it was still being spoken. But he makes many allusions to Jesus' teaching, especially in the Sermon on the Mount, and to Paul's teaching, for Paul had been the main protagonist in the council of Jerusalem because of his work among the Gentiles. So James was a man of prayer and a man of scripture who suffered that most appalling death. I have given you that background because that is the man who wrote this letter, and I think that gives you a respect for him and an interest in him because of what he was.

Let us move from the writer to the readers. There can be

little doubt as to who they were. The letter is addressed to the twelve tribes scattered among the nations. The Hebrew word for scattered is "Dispersed" or "Diaspora". There had been two scatterings of the Jewish people among the nations. One was compulsory and the other was voluntary. It is to these people that James is writing. Therefore it is a letter from a Messianic Jew. Just to go back for a moment to what he calls himself now, he says, "I'm a slave of God and of the Lord Jesus Christ." That is a very unusual thing to say. For one thing, it puts God and Jesus on the same pedestal – "I'm a slave of him and him", putting them as equals. Notice the word "slave". It is translated in some Bibles as "servant" because we are not familiar with slavery, but it is the word "slave". He had been bought; a price had been paid for him. Paul called himself "the bond slave of Jesus". They were bought and therefore belonged totally to God and to the Lord Jesus Christ.

Pause for a moment and look at those three words. "Lord" – the only person called "lord" in the Roman Empire was Caesar. But the early Christians immediately applied that to Jesus. Their first creed was "Jesus is Lord". Still to this day it is only Christians who use that title of Jesus. If you hear someone talk about the Lord Jesus you know they are a believer in the Saviour. The world does not call Jesus "Lord". It is the highest title that could be given. The early Christians paid the price for calling Jesus "Lord".

Once a year, on what was called the "Lord's Day", or the "Lordy Day", everybody had to appear before a statue of Caesar and an altar to Caesar. They had to throw incense on the altar and stand before the bust of Caesar, raise their right hand and say "Caesar is Lord". If they refused, they died. It was the first big test of Christian faithfulness. They refused to say "Caesar is Lord". They said, "No, there's only one person who deserves that title – Jesus is Lord." They said it in the church and they said it outside the church, and that was very dangerous.

So we know this man is a Messianic Jew. He calls Jesus Lord and "Christ". The word "Christ" is not Jesus' surname. That is what it has become for Christians and we just say "Christ" as if it is a name. It means king. It means king of the Jews. It is the Greek form of the Hebrew word meaning "anointed" (Hebrew, *Maschiah*) Messiah, the anointed king. Therefore, we ought to be saying "King Jesus". That would convey to people what we really mean: "The Lord Jesus, King of the Jews", and one day of the whole world. So it is a very important word. Here is this man willing to die now for his half-brother, willing to say openly: "I am a slave of the Lord Jesus Christ." Those words sum up his faith.

He is writing to the twelve tribes in the Dispersion who also are Jews. I have already mentioned that there were two exiles from their land. The first began six hundred years earlier, when the Assyrians took ten tribes away, and later when the Babylonians came and took the other two, so that the whole nation had been taken into exile compulsorily, because God was behind it. It was God who brought the Assyrians to the ten tribes in the north, called Israel. It was God who brought the Babylonians to deal with the two left in the south (one was Benjamin, the other Judah) and to take them away. So that exile in Assyria first and then Babylon was God's punishment for his people. He had warned them again and again through prophets: you go on disobeying me and living your own way and you will lose the land I promised. They should have been in no doubt as to what happened.

It is an interesting aside that once every seven years they had been told to give the land a rest, letting it lie fallow. For five hundred years they refused to do that and went on cropping the land every year, giving it no rest. The result of that was that the land did not have a holiday for seventy years in total. So God told them: if you won't give the land a holiday, I will; out you go. The land became fallow and rested for seventy years. That is how Daniel knew when the time was up to go back, and they came back – or at least some of them did. Most stayed in Babylon; about forty-five thousand came home, resettled the land and rebuilt the temple.

But a hundred years before Christ came there had been a second exile, a second dispersion, this time a voluntary one. Why? Because the whole empire had opened up. The empire had roads leading to every part. The empire had one language, a *lingua franca*, so they could go anywhere and they could speak anywhere. That resulted in a voluntary exodus from the Promised Land for thousands of Jews. Ten thousand of them made a home in Rome. But if you re-read the account of Pentecost in Acts 2, read about some of the countries where they went. Why did they go? I can give you the answer in one word – money.

They went to trade. They went to do business. Jews are pretty good at that; they are shrewd people and each of them has an ambition to have his own business. So they went down the Roman roads. They traded, and they virtually took over the trade of the Roman Empire. Some of them were successful and made a lot of money and some of them were failures and did not. The result was that outside the land the gap between rich and poor became wider and wider. So you had rich Jewish businessmen in posh houses, and nearby you had poor Jews living in shanty towns. That is why James is constantly mentioning rich and poor in his letter, and he is very much against the rich, as we will see.

So the Jews who had scattered and left the land had gone for business and trading, and had been doing that in the Dispersion ever since. Notice that none of the tribes has been lost. We hear so much talk about the lost tribes of Israel. Some people think that Britain and America are the successors of the lost tribes of Israel. No, tribes were never lost. God, who knows the number of hairs on your head, must know your DNA inside out. He knows the DNA of every living human being and he must know, therefore, where his ancient people have gone. He is calling all of them back now from the twelve tribes. The latest tribe to come back is Manasseh. Did you follow the return of the Manasseh tribe from India? Only fairly recently – that is the latest to come back.

James is therefore writing to the twelve tribes who are scattered among the nations. Not scattered by God this time, but by their own greed and their own ability to do business. It is also true that he is writing to Messianic Jews in the Dispersion. He treats them throughout the letter as Christians. He makes reference to Christian belief, and the whole thing is a Christian letter, from a Christian to a Christian. But they would not have called themselves that. That word, "Christian", was used only of Gentiles in the New Testament. If they were alive today they would call themselves "Messianic Jews".

So this letter is from a Messianic Jew to Messianic Jews who are scattered among the nations. That raises an immediate question: then why on earth are Gentiles now reading it? Why on earth should we study James, written by a Messianic Jew to Messianic Jews? The answer is really very simple: we are in the same boat – we are aliens in an alien world. We are strangers, we are pilgrims, we are just passing through – our citizenship is in heaven. We don't belong here, but we find ourselves here because we were born here. Therefore we are God's people scattered among the nations. The same temptations they had, we have. The biggest temptation of scattered Jews is to assimilate, becoming too like the world around them, adopting the customs and the culture of Gentile nations. We, too, find that our biggest problem. It is called in the New Testament "worldliness". We will see that James says a lot about the world in his letter, and not to follow the world, not to be conformed to it, not to become worldly inside us, because worldliness is not just what you do outside, it is what you are inside. So we have all the pressures, temptations and problems of the twelve tribes scattered among the nations. That is why we read this book and why it is one of the most relevant and important books for Christians to study.

We have looked at the writer and looked at the readers and we have realised how relevant all this is to us. By way of comparison, at the beginning of 1 Peter the writer is talking to Gentile Christians yet he uses the terms of a Jewish Diaspora – of Gentile believers. He said, "To God's elect, chosen, strangers in the world, scattered throughout Pontus, Galatia, Cappadocia, Asia and Bithynia," all of which are in modern Turkey, by the way. This is the Christian Diaspora, the Christian Gentiles scattered among the nations. These are the pressures we all face. So James becomes a most relevant letter to the Christian Diaspora.

So we are now looking at the twelve tribes scattered among the nations and I have given you their story first. In their voluntary dispersion they went down the trade routes to do business, to make money, and therefore they were driven to this exile through greed. Therefore, their number one problem was wealth – those who had made money and those who had not, and the tension between them.

Had they still been in their own land it would not have been a problem because every fiftieth year there was a levelling out of society by God's law and land had to be given back to its original owner. Slaves had to be set free. Debts were cancelled. It was called the Jubilee year. That meant that in a sense everybody went back to the same as they began with, every fifty years. It was a revolutionary idea in society. Can you imagine our government doing that, so that all our money is levelled off every fifty years and all the debts cancelled and all the property restored to the original owner? Great idea—and it was God's idea to prevent a great gap between rich and poor developing. But of course the Jubilee was practised in the land, not in the Dispersion. That is where Jews could either be very rich or, by failure, very poor, and that is where the gap appeared. That gap is mentioned four times in that letter. In some countries today the gap between rich and poor is widening. There is no Jubilee every fifty years to level everybody off again. It is worth thinking through the implications of that in politics.

Now that was the first concern, and the second was gossip. A preacher told his congregation: "I will now show you that part of my body with which I have most difficulty in overcoming temptation." The congregation became breathless and waited to see what he would do. What he did was to stick his tongue out! We learn a lot in the letter of James about speech and the sins of speech and how we can control our tongues. I have been in places overseas where there is a particular kind of little British colony of immigrants. When they are together it is gossip, gossip – because it is a very small community and they all know each other very well, too well. The tongue can become a real problem in exile.

The third problem they had was divisions among them. I don't know if you have heard the Jewish proverb "Two Jews; three opinions." I am afraid there is truth in that. There is a joke about two Jews wrecked on a desert island and they build three synagogues. One goes to one, another goes to another, and the third is the synagogue they would not be seen dead in! Such jokes came to me from Jews. They recognise themselves and their own weakness. James is going to point out the difference between cleverness or worldly wisdom, which splits people up, and the wisdom that is from above, which brings people together. Of course he was a perfect example of the latter.

The fourth difficulty they had, and the major one, was assimilation, becoming like the people around them, adopting the culture of Gentiles. This is what happened in Germany before World War I. The German Jews were becoming so assimilated and they were running the banks, the theatres, the universities, and I don't know what else in Germany. They had become more German than Jewish. God sent them at least two prophets to tell them. One of them was a Jew called Jabotinsky. He travelled around the Jews of Europe saying, "Destroy the Diaspora before it destroys you." In other words, "Get out now!" He was doing this around 1900, and he foresaw the Holocaust so clearly. He tried to warn the Jewish people to get out while they could. But they did not listen, and he died in utter poverty in New York, a broken man.

Then there was Theodor Herzl, who from 1897 was pleading with Jews to have their own Promised Land and not stay in Germany. People do not realise that God never does anything harmful without warning people first, telling them first. The story of the prophets who told the Jews of Europe to get out at the beginning of the twentieth century, fifty years before the Holocaust, is there for all to read.

So there is this problem of assimilation, and we still talk about British people who have "gone native", who have moved overseas and then become more and more like the people they are living among. We have our diplomats and our councils and our ambassadors. Their first duty is to remain true to their home country and not to go native. But when you are surrounded by them, it is so easy. It is so easy – we have to live among unbelievers, work among them, mix with them, and we ought to. But gradually that can get hold of us and take us away from our unique citizenship in heaven.

That is enough about the readers of this letter. Now let us notice a few things about the letter itself. It has a name and address, the name of the sender and the address of the receiver, right at the beginning. That makes it a letter. But for the rest it is not like a letter at all, it is like a sermon. There are no references to any people by name. There are no references to places by name. Above all, it does not begin with any congratulations. It was a common practice of letters of those days, followed by most of the letters in the New Testament, to compliment the people, saying something nice about them before you said something nasty.

It is a good habit, and Paul's letters display that, though he was not a flatterer. There is only one of his letters where he could find nothing good to say about the people first, and that is Galatians. But in every other letter he congratulates them on something good before he weighs in with criticism. Jesus did the same with the seven letters he dictated to the seven churches in Asia. But there were two that he could not find anything good to say about, and there were also two that he had nothing bad to say about.

So the epistle has the form of the letter, the name and address, but nothing else. When Paul finished off a letter he always gave greetings to people he knew – friends. But there are no greetings in James. So for the rest, there is very little of a letter about this letter. It is going to be circulated around a group of people, so its form is what we call a "circular letter", such as we get at Christmas from many people. Though it is addressed personally you know perfectly well it has gone to many others. Being guilty myself, I send out about three hundred news letters. I try to make them personal, but they can't be. They have to be general.

There is a combination of two styles: Hebrew and Greek.

This is astonishing because James came from humble beginnings in Israel, yet he has mastered the Greek language and the Greek culture to such an extent that you don't know when you are reading this letter whether you are reading a Hebrew letter or what is called a Greek "diatribe" or lecture. So we have the best of both worlds. Let us take the Hebrew wisdom. Why can't James talk in linear fashion? Because he talks in circular fashion, he keeps coming back to a subject, moves on again; comes back to it, moves on again.

So for someone like me who loves to analyse things, and especially books of the Bible – I can't. There is no overall structure such as just about every letter Paul wrote has. A typical "Hebrew thinking" letter would be Ephesians: chapters 1–3 is on Christian belief, and chapters 4–6 on Christian behaviour. I like that. My mind likes the clear structure. But I can't do that with James, he just goes round and round. What does that remind you of? Well, it reminds me of the Book of Proverbs. When you read Proverbs it does just the same thing, jumping from one subject to another, and coming back to a subject. It is all jumbled up. It is typical of a Jewish rabbi.

In fact the Jews have a name for it, *charaz*, which means this kind of wandering wisdom that just pours out on all kinds of different subjects. That is the letter of James. There is some structure in smaller sections of it, but I can't give you an analysis of the whole book. It just doesn't fit that way. So it is very much like the Hebrew prophets, thoroughly Hebrew in fact. But it is also very Greek. The language is superb Greek, so much so that some people have doubted whether James could have written it. He could have had a secretary, an "amanuensis", as Paul used Silas. I don't know. I prefer to believe that James had really studied Greek and knew it as well as any Greek. He is writing to Jews in the Diaspora who all had to speak Greek. So you have a superb

Greek piece of oratory. I made a list of eleven features of a Greek speech. Greeks loved oratory; they used to listen to lectures for hours on Mars Hill.

First, he uses rhetorical questions. That means when you ask an audience something but don't want the answer. As the preacher in the City Temple in London once said, "You, young men in the gallery, would you rather spend eternity with wise virgins in the light or with the foolish ones in the dark?" That was a rhetorical question but he got a unanimous answer he didn't expect from the young men in the gallery.

There are others: using paradox or irony to get attention. There is having an imaginary debate with an imaginary objector. James does that. There is using a question to introduce a new subject. That is a familiar device. Imperative commands, figures of speech, personification – where you take an abstract idea and imagine it in a person. There is using famous men and women to illustrate your point. There is the direct address: "you; you; you". There is the use of strong language. Above all, there is antithesis where you make contrasts: black/white; rich/poor; good/bad. There is also use of apt quotations from others. Those were some ways that Greek orators used to keep an audience interested and in touch. James uses all those. So here you have the best of both worlds. You have the height of Hebrew wisdom matched with Greek skill with speech.

Finally, in this introduction, we look at the contents. It is important to realise that it is an *ethical* letter. What do I mean by that? In Ephesians (for example) Christian belief came first and then the Christian ethics or the morality came second. There is none of that in James. There is a little about justification in chapter two, which is the most argued about in the whole letter. But there is not a clear division. There is very little doctrine here. There is very little teaching on salvation. All of it is on the practical side of working out what God is working in.

There is a lot about God in it, especially about him as Judge, but no systematic doctrine. There is a tremendous emphasis on *doing* it. The key word in this letter is the two-letter word "Do". That is a word that we often ignore in scripture. It is a little word but probably the most important word. I was trying to think of a title for the whole of James. The one that most people preferred was "Now Do It". I think that sums up James. It is a workout for Christians. We are told in Philippians: "Work out your salvation, for it is God who works in you." It takes the second part for granted.

James has taken completely for granted that he is writing to Christians who have been justified by faith and who must now be taught how to do it, how to apply it. This brings me to why people find scripture difficult. When people find difficulties in the Bible I divide them in my mind into two groups: those who find it difficult to understand and those who don't. Most people's problem with scripture is what they do understand but don't do. So you can say about every problem of scripture that either some people can't apprehend it or it is something they are unwilling to apply, and with James the latter is the issue.

As we go through the letter we shall be challenged very deeply to *do* it, to apply it, to ask the question: what does that say to me? One of the points that James will make is this: don't be a sermon taster, don't go home and have roast preacher for lunch. When you listen to the Word of God, don't judge the speaker; let the Word of God judge you.

2
TRIALS AND TEMPTATIONS

Read James 1:2–18

A. TESTED (2-12) – by external
    1. Great rejoicing (2-8)
        a. Perseverance
        b. Perception
    2. Great Reversal (9-11)
        a. Poor – High
        b. Rich – Low
    3. Great reward (12)
        a. Life – what?
        b. Love – who?
B. TEMPTED (13-18) – by internal
    1. Bad passions from within (13-15)
        a. Desire – conception
        b. Disobedience – birth
        c. Decease – death
    2. Good presents from above (16-18)
        a. Truth – not deception
        b. Birth – not death

When I was a new Christian I was fascinated to listen to testimonies of other Christians. One thing that troubled me about those testimonies was that so many of them said something like this: I came to Jesus and all my troubles were over. I thought: why is my testimony not like that? Mine is just the opposite! I came to Jesus and all my troubles began.

Then I got filled with the Spirit and all my troubles got worse, and I have been in more trouble in the last ten years than the previous thirty. So my testimony was rather different. But I was comforted when I read Jesus' words: "In the world you shall have big trouble. But cheer up, I'm on top of it."

I was reminded of a friend of mine, when I asked him, "How are you?" He replied, "I'm very well over the circumstances!" Most people are "under" the circumstances, but he said "over them", and only a Christian could say that. Let us look at this word "trouble" or "tribulation". It comes from the Latin *tribulum*, which was the description of a threshing sledge. That is a big square of wood, and on the underneath flint stones have been embedded in holes, and that is dragged over the corn by a donkey. It is a vivid description. When you have trouble you feel like that sometimes, as if you have been dragged over by sharp stones, as if everything is against you.

Here we have a Greek word (*peirasmos*) used by James, but it is a bit ambiguous, with two very different meanings. On the one hand it means *trials*, on the other hand it means *temptations*. Yet these two things are very different. Trials come from outside. Adverse circumstances, all sorts of things, make life rough and tough for Christians from the outside. Whereas James is going to tell us that temptation comes from the inside and the problem must be dealt with inside you. Trials come to everybody, and they come to Christians more than to others. This is mainly because we are in an alien world. We don't belong here, we don't fit. We become social misfits when we belong to Christ, and therefore we have adverse circumstances built in. But the other problem is that we were born into that world, we were part of it, and we only got out of it through Christ.

Therefore we have this internal problem of temptations which come from our old life, from our former habits;

habits of behaviour, habits of thinking, habits of feeling, and they are still there. It is what the Bible calls the "old man". The problem is that the old man is dead but he won't lie down. We all have problems with "the flesh", as it is called – what we were born with and what we did with that flesh in the early years of our life. So James is dealing with this one Greek word *peirasmos*, which we could translate "pressures". Some of the pressures come from outside (what James calls trials) and some of them come from the inside (what he calls temptations).

He tells us how to deal with them. The first thing he says is a surprise: "Count it all joy when you suffer many trials." Now that is not advice the world will give you. The world will tell you to try to avoid those trials but to do everything you can not to come into adverse circumstances. Many people succeed in not having too hard a life. So what James says is amazing. Notice that he does not say enjoy trials. Thank God for that, because it is not easy to enjoy adverse circumstances. But he does say rejoice in them.

That is a very different thing. It is something that comes from your mind rather than your heart. Nobody "feels" like enjoying adverse circumstances, but your mind can have a different attitude. Your mind can say "Put it on the joy side, count it all joy, reckon it all joy." We have got to do that a lot in the Christian life. When you don't feel like something, reckon, count, let your mind rule your heart. So we are to count it all joy when things go wrong. That is marvellous counsel but not easy advice. I think of Paul in prison in Rome, yet if you read the letter he wrote from Rome called Philippians, the word "joy" comes in again and again, finishing with: "Rejoice always!" Here is a man under house arrest facing possible execution and he was saying count it all joy. I think of another man called Paul – Paul Schneider, a great hero of mine who was a pastor in a suburb of Berlin. He dared to preach against Hitler, who was coming to power. I have his life story and his letters to his wife after he was taken off to Dachau. The Gestapo came for him at three in the morning and he was starved to death in the concentration camp. I went to the church where he was pastor, in the suburbs of Berlin. His widow still attended. His letters to his wife and family while he was starved to death are full of the word "joy" and gratitude.

There are many saints you could illustrate this from, who, because they believed in Jesus, have rejoiced when things were against them, when they were suffering. They could not have suffered more, some of them, and yet they came through rejoicing. It is a command to count it all joy. We are to do that. So why such rejoicing? The answer is, first, that it produces perseverance. I like to ask people if they know my friend Percy, whose surname is Verance! Every Christian needs to be acquainted with Percy. You do it by counting all adverse circumstances joy, for your benefit.

So, on suffering, I put it this way: a hard life makes you hearty. That is positive, progress, improvement. So don't grumble when your circumstances are against you. When everything seems to go wrong say, "I put that in the joy column and it is for my good. It is going to do wonders for my character." People who don't suffer much don't grow much, have you noticed that? You find in every mature saint suffering of some kind. They have been through it and they have come through it and they have passed the test, for trials are a test of the kind of people we are. Do we just grumble and complain? That is what the world does when things go wrong. We don't. We count it all joy.

It says here that God wants to make you complete – a complete Christian, lacking nothing. His objective for every one of us is perfection, maturity. But many Christians remain baby Christians; they have not learned perseverance.

They have not learned how to be reliable people whom you can trust, stable Christians who don't cave in when things go badly for them. So God's will is fully-fashioned men and women of God who have this unique quality called perseverance. Furthermore, James says you need perception as well as perseverance. You need wisdom, in other words – wisdom to know what is going on, wisdom to understand what is happening to you, wisdom to know the right reaction to have.

Where do you get it? The world gets it from education and experience. But Christians don't get it from there, because that is worldly wisdom. The Bible is not written to make you worldly wise. It is not written to make you clever. It is not written to make you rich. It is written to make you wise unto salvation, and that is a very different thing. Where do we get wisdom from? The answer is from God. He is described in my New Testament as the only wise God. It is his wisdom that is available to us. This is the amazing truth that James reveals now: if you want wisdom, go to the right place: ask, and you will get it. It is as simple as that.

Why is it as simple as that? First, because God is generous. He loves giving to people what they need. He responds to a request for help. When you say, "Lord, I don't understand what's happening; it all seems to be going wrong," that is the very point where you need to ask for wisdom. Say, "Lord, I want your wisdom, to see what you think about this, to see things from your point of view." He will give it generously. It says he gives it without finding fault in you. If you go to some people for help they will say, "Right, I'll give you some help. But I do need to say you're doing this wrong." Or, "I could give you more help if you would do this." When God gives, he gives unconditionally without finding fault, without criticising you. I find that amazing because God could criticise me so easily. He could say, "I'll give you help if you put this right, if you'll do that." But he doesn't, he gives it generously. That is how we become wise people. You don't become wise through any other way but simply asking. That is what Solomon did. When he came to the throne God said, "I'll give you anything you ask for; I'll give you riches, I'll give you power, I'll give you anything you want." Solomon said, "There's only one thing I want – wisdom." The next morning he really needed it. Two women were arguing over one baby; they had both had babies, one had died and now both were claiming the survivor. What wisdom a man would need, faced with that! You can imagine. He got it, and he said, "Cut the baby in half and give half to each woman." As soon as he said that, one of the women said, "No! Don't! Give it to the other." He said, "You're the woman aren't you? You're the mother." What wisdom, and because he had asked for it he got it. We can ask for it and we can get it. We will perceive things from God's point of view, see things as he sees them. When everything is going against us we will understand and say, "Thank you, Lord. I didn't see it that way."

So on his side there is no barrier. He is wanting to give it, willing to give it freely. No fault-finding; no criticism. But on our side there could be a hang up. This is the first time that James has mentioned prayer. He is going to say there is one thing that blocks prayer, and it is doubt. If you are going to ask God for anything, don't ever doubt that he will give it, because if you doubt you are like a wave of the sea tossed by the wind.

You will have stood by the seashore and watched a wave come rolling in, and you see the wind turn it into spray. That wave will be gone; a minute later it will not be there. It is only breaking into a wave because it has reached the shallow shore and has become unstable. It was a steady ripple in the ocean until it hit the shallows. Then it came up, the wind caught it, and it was gone. That is what a person is like who prays with doubts. Here is a very big challenge: when you ask God for something you must be sure that he will give it.

Now there are other conditions, which James will mention later, for unanswered prayer. But the first is: don't doubt. He says an amazing thing: a man who doubts when he prays will be unstable in everything else. So your prayer life is a guide to the rest of your life. If you doubt there, and if you are shaken there, then you will be a ditherer in everything else in your life. That is the first big challenge of James: dithering, doubting, shaken, just a wave of the sea, here and gone. That is the first nature simile he has used.

I label that passage "The Great Rejoicing". "The Great", because you will not find anybody else rejoicing in adverse circumstances, but with us you should. The second thing he writes about could be called "The Great Reversal". He now tackles this problem of the rich and poor, where the gap is getting greater and some of the Jewish businessmen are making a fortune and others are making nothing at all. Again, it is a surprising reversal. It needs divine wisdom to discern who is better off in life, and it is not the rich. It is the poor. The world will not agree with that at all. The world says the people who are "better" off in life are the rich. It is true that they can use their money to reduce adverse circumstances and avoid them even, but they are not to be congratulated – far from it.

He begins with the poor and says, "Let the poor take pride in their low position." That is not popular politics but it is what Jesus said. "Woe to you rich and blessed are you poor...." He gave reasons for it. He said, "Woe to you rich, because you've had all the comfort you're going to get here. And blessed are you poor, for yours is the kingdom of heaven." We find all the way through that James is reversing the world's opinions. He is talking about what some have called the "upside down culture" of the Christian. I think it is right way up. But it has rightly been called by the world the upside down culture, because they see it from their upside down position. So to them we are upside down.

But actually, from God's point of view, you are right way up. The poor should be taking pride in their situation. What amazing advice! In other words, let's face it, too many people think that wealth or prosperity is a sign of God's blessing and that poverty is a sign of his curse. There are an increasing number of preachers today all over the world who are saying, "Prosperity is God's blessing and poverty is God's cursing." I am sure you have heard of the prosperity gospel which is catching on worldwide at the moment. But that is not what James says. James is teaching: you poor, take pride in your low position; you should be proud of being poor. That is divine wisdom. James does not explain here why the poor person is in a high position, he takes it for granted that we know. He says: you know this. But he does explain why the rich are in a low position, and their low position is that it is soon gone and they will lose it so suddenly. On the whole, poor people have more adverse circumstances than rich people. As I have observed, wealth can be a kind of cushion against life. You can always pay for a doctor or a dentist or whatever. But money only protects you for a time. Years ago I was invited to preach at the Stock Exchange in London to the stockbrokers. They asked for a subject to advertise and so I sent them this: "You Can't Take It With You, And If You Could It Would Burn." They didn't like that title at all. They said, "You've got to change that title." So I did change it to: "How to Invest Your Money Beyond the Grave" and told them all: you are all saving up for your pension, for your retirement, for when you can do what you want instead of what you are being told. But I then said: "It's a very short-term policy because you are going to leave it all behind." A shroud has no pockets. When a wealthy man died, somebody said, "How much did he leave?" The answer was, "Everything." That is the truth. The rich man relies more and more on his riches. It means so much to him and he is going to lose it all – as the flower fades, says James, when the hot scorching sun hits it. That is the rich man. That is his real position. It is a very low position, a very insecure position. In other words, the poor have so much more to gain and the rich have so much more to lose. That is the real outlook for these two groups. James says that is God's point of view. He said the rich man will lose everything even while he is pursuing his wealth, even while he is doing business.

My mind goes back to a dinner in a London hotel which I was invited to attend with businessmen. Certainly, looking around, they were successful businessmen. Suddenly, in the middle of dinner, a man at the next table of eight people had a fatal heart attack, and was gone and he was carried out of the dinner. All his wealth was no use to him. Right in the middle of a superb hotel reception and a good meal – that brought home to me what James says here. The rich man's position is very precarious. This is a real reversal of fortune, and it is one that we should remember.

Paul Getty lived half a mile from us, and I always thought of him as rich. By comparison I was poor. We tend, if we are not careful, to think like that, to compare ourselves with people who are richer than we are. So we don't think of ourselves as rich. But by New Testament standards, the majority of people in developed countries today are rich. By Jesus' standards we are the rich who will find it difficult to get into the kingdom because we are comfortably off. Even the unemployed in this country are better off than employed people in Jesus' day. They have a television they can watch, and that is luxury. So let us not fall into the trap of thinking that we are neither rich nor poor. We are rich if we are comfortably off. Therefore we can turn away adverse circumstances for the most part. We have the means to pay someone to overcome for us. But it is the poor who are in the high position. Notice that James says the same to both: take pride in your position. The poor should take pride in their high position, and the rich should take pride in their low position, and then they can both praise God for something. Again, to the world it is contrary advice.

Poor people are much more open to help, much more open to the gospel. Where is the gospel being most listened to today? The answer is in the Far East – and in the southern hemisphere, especially in poorer parts of the world. Churches are not growing fantastically here because we are well-off. But they are growing in Africa and southeast Asia, and South America. That is where there is growth because people who are poor are more open to the gospel. Rich people say, "I'm comfortably off, I don't need God. I've got everything I need. I don't need anything else." That is why there is such a growing gap between the two. But for the poor there is a great reward waiting at the end of the line. James draws from the Olympic Games in Ancient Greece. When a person won a game he was crowned with a ring of laurel leaves. That was the crown, something put round their forehead. That is what James is thinking of here – a crown waiting for those who love the Lord. On the whole it is poor people who love the Lord more than rich people. Therefore he says there is a crown waiting for them. It is a crown of life.

There has been a big debate among theological scholars on whether "eternal life" means quantity – everlasting – or a matter of quality, abundant life? I think it is a silly debate because it is both. It is a life of more quantity than this life, and it is a life of more quality. The two together make it life. That is waiting at the end of the race for those who love God.

So much then for what *trials* can do to us. Let us now

move to the *temptations*. This is quite a different meaning but the matter is complicated in that the same Greek word (*peirasmos*) does for both meanings (trials and temptations) in English. So here the same word is used again, but now meaning temptations.

Temptations come from the inside of us (even when Satan tempts us he is latching on to a decision within), whereas trials come from outside us and we cannot stop them. We can stop temptation, and James tells us how. It is not only inside but it is negative as well, whereas trials are positive. After all, tests are good for you. Every pilot is tested. Every athlete is tested. Every student is tested. Such tests are meant to be positive, to improve the candidate, to help them to succeed. With a test there is always the hope that you will succeed. A temptation, however, is just the opposite. Temptation plays on your weakness. A trial plays on your strengths and will make you even better, and result in perseverance and patience, whereas a temptation is to put you down. So there is a huge difference.

James makes a categorical statement about God here: he cannot be tempted and does not tempt anyone else. Let us look at two other scriptures in the light of what James writes, as some have said James is contradicting other scriptures here. Throughout the law of Moses, tempting God is forbidden. "You shall not tempt the Lord your God" is found four times in the law. Yet here James is telling his readers that you can't tempt God – so why try? When Jesus was tempted to throw himself off that pinnacle of the temple, he said, "It is written: 'Don't tempt the Lord your God.'"

So what is James saying here? He is saying this: "Don't tempt the Lord your God as you did at Massah". What did the people of Israel do in Massah that was said to be tempting God? The answer is that they grumbled for lack of water. They came to Moses and said, "Is God with us or not? We want to have proof that he is with us. Let him give us water, because we need water." That is tempting the Lord our God. How? It is asking for more assurance than God is willing to give you. It is putting him to the test, to see whether he is really involved. It is easy to do that. You can get a church praying like mad for a member of the church who is ill, and it could be tempting the Lord our God unless you have a clear revelation from the Lord that he wants to heal the person and he is going to. Just praying for the sick is tempting him, testing him. "Oh God, if you're there, do this...." We are told not to do that, and some people try. It is a case of wanting more certainty in your life than he has been willing to give you. It is doubting him. It is praying like a wave tossed by the wind when you say: "God, I want proof that you're here. I want proof that your promises are true." It is asking him for proof. It is not really a temptation, it is a test. Many modern versions have translated that prohibition, "Do not put the Lord to the test." People do that, and it is usually a sign of lack of faith in God. If they really believe God they would be sure. They wouldn't want him to "prove" himself to them.

Now what about those scriptures that say that? Think of the Lord's Prayer, which we are supposed to pray every day as believers. In that prayer is, "Lead us not into temptation." But James says that God doesn't tempt anyone. So how do we reconcile those scriptures, James and the Lord's Prayer? Well, let's look at it very closely. Let's complete the petition. "When you pray," said Jesus, "go into your room by yourself and pray, 'Our Father ... give us....'" That is an interesting insight – there is no such thing as private prayer; you are part of the Body even when you are by yourself. There is the petition: "Lead us not into temptation, but deliver us from the evil one." What a pity that the Lord's Prayer was not properly translated. It is not "Deliver us from evil." Evil does not exist. It is not a *thing* that exists by itself. It can only exist in person. So we must not think of evil as some vague, black thing that is in the world. There are only evil persons, and at the head of them is one very evil person, which the Bible refers to as "the evil one". So the Lord's Prayer, as we call it, is a prayer that Jesus would never pray himself – he didn't need to. But he told us to pray. It begins with the Father in heaven and it ends with Satan, and it is a daily prayer: don't lead us into temptation, but deliver us from the evil one, from the devil. The part about the kingdom, the power and the glory was added later, it was not in Jesus' original teaching.

So the prayer that he taught us begins with the Father and ends with the devil, and that is how it should be. The second thing to note is that it does not say God tempts us, but he can lead us into temptation. It says of Jesus, after his baptism, that the Holy Spirit led him into the wilderness to be tempted by the devil. So God can lead you into temptation, though he doesn't ever tempt anyone. Do you follow me? He can expose you to Satan. That is what we are asking in the Lord's Prayer that he doesn't do. Let us take that a bit further. Why should God lead us into temptation? The answer is a salutary lesson to us.

Let us go to another text in 1 Corinthians 10:13 – "He will never let you be tempted above your capacity to refuse." In other words, God controls our temptations rigidly. Here is a promise to a believer: "I will not let you be tempted above what you can bear." As Paul says in one of his letters, he has given us the grace to say no – which means that a Christian who sins has no excuse whatever for sinning. If God has controlled my temptations from the devil, only allowing through those that I can handle, then I am completely responsible for giving way. Yet many of us try to make excuses. We try to blame someone else or our circumstances. But we cannot do that. As Christians we have to admit, "I didn't say no; I said yes, and I have no excuse for doing that."

So God controls our temptations, but if we persistently say yes then he will lead us to more temptation to teach us a lesson. That is what the church itself is called to do in the New Testament. The church can deliver someone to Satan as a last resort, and it is a last resort. But if you can do nothing else to correct a believer who is bringing the gospel into disgrace you can deliver them to Satan, and they will then suffer his temptations – and deserts. It could lead to sickness and death. When you are praying the Lord's Prayer you are saying to God: please don't use that last resort. Because when Paul told the Church of Corinth to deliver to Satan the man who was having sex with his mother, he told the church: you are doing that to save him; you are doing that for his hope. You are doing that so that he will be saved in the last day. It is a redemptive, saving thing to do to deliver someone to Satan. That puts a whole new light on things. I am dealing with something quite seriously now. I have known churches that delivered people to Satan and I have seen the results of that. It is saying: Satan, do your worst with this man to bring him to his senses. Praise God, in 2 Corinthians you find that it did the trick. Paul says, "The majority of you put him out of fellowship, now all of you welcome him back in because he's repented." One of the missing factors in so many churches today is discipline. Of course it is not easy to apply when, if you apply discipline to a member, they just trot down the road and start attending another church, and the other church does nothing about it. Let me plead with any pastors that when you discipline a member inform the other churches that they are disciplined. Other churches, if they are wise, will not take them in.

Let us look more closely at what happens inside us when temptation comes. I know temptations come from the devil and from the world and from the flesh, which is our old life. But they couldn't get in if there wasn't something in us that wanted it. Every fisherman has bait, and it may be a fly or it may be part of a little fish, but he is putting on the hook something that the other fish will want. If there wasn't that desire within the fish, no bait would work. Trout love flies. So they make incredible flies to fish the river. Satan can't touch you unless there is something in you that wants it. That is why he is putting the emphasis on what is inside.

It is a brilliant analysis now of how sin gets hold of us. It begins with the conception of sin. It is like the ordinary life cycle. Conception begins it, birth settles that, and as soon as you are born you are on the road to death. That is inevitable. That is physical life. James is teaching that temptation is just the same. It is conceived internally, in the mind, it is played with in the imagination. It couldn't start if you didn't welcome it. So the first step of temptation is conception, and that happens invisibly inside. Other people may be totally unaware of it happening, but that is where it begins.

That is why Jesus said both murder and adultery begin in the mind, in the heart. They begin with wanting something you don't have. You can't stop birds flying over your head, but you can stop them from nesting in your hair – that is an old proverb. I don't know where it came from, but it is right. What the proverb means is that it is not a sin to be tempted. What happens is that when you conceive it, it goes into the mind and you imagine it happening. Many people are an accident waiting to happen. They have not actually sinned outside. Nobody knows that they have already conceived it, but it is there in their mind. They imagine it, they want it. They do it inside before they do it outside, and that is Jesus' teaching which James is passing on to us. Don't let that conception take place. The way to deal with sin is not abortion but contraception, if you understand my meaning. The time to deal with sin is when the first thought is there. You entertain it and it stays; it develops. It may be nine months before it comes out. It may be longer before it actually happens, but it is there already, waiting to be born. That is where it starts, in the world of fantasy. Then it goes on to birth, and that is actual disobedience, and you know you have done wrong when you have done it. But in fact, you have prepared the way for it.

Therefore, you were an accident waiting to happen and you cannot stop it happening now. Conception gives way to birth, inevitably. Then the disobedience comes out. Through life it may be occasional at first, but then it becomes regular, and then it becomes habitual. Very soon it has become part of your living character. Now this is a brilliant diagnosis of how sin gets into your life. Of course the wages of sin is death, so as soon as it is birthed you are heading for death. As soon as you were born in this world you were certain to die, and every one of your heartbeats is like a drum rolling on your pilgrimage to death. It is the same with sin. It will grow and grow, becoming more and more part of your character, more and more difficult to resist, more and more difficult to change, until finally it kills you. Every one of us is going to die. We are all going to face it because we have all been sinners. So we can understand James' diagnosis of how sin gets hold of us. There must be some wrong desires, some bad passions within which can play with an idea and do it in imagination over and over again, until finally conception produces birth, and birth produces death – a brilliant diagnosis of which we need to take notice.

In v. 12 we saw the crown of life as the end product of those who love God; here it is death that is the wages and the result. Finally, James says about God the opposite of his opening statement, "Let no one say, 'I'm tempted by God.'" The Father of lights, heavenly lights, sun, moon, and stars, in him is no darkness. Furthermore, there is no shadow of turning in God.

The only two things we have had from heaven are, first of all, our new birth and, second, the truth. Our new birth came about through the truth, and it was because we knew the truth from his Word that we found new birth, new life, a second life. We Christians are the firstfruits of a whole new creation. God is making new people first and a new heaven and a new earth last. That is the opposite way around from Genesis, where he made the heaven and the earth first and people last.

God is getting people ready for the second creation. We are living in the eighth day of creation. God has gone back to work. He went back to work on the day of Christ's resurrection. The first bit of the old creation that he made new was Jesus' own body, and he became the firstfruits, as he is called in the New Testament. We are now new men and women – prepared, or being prepared, for a new heaven and a new earth. God will not allow any of us into that new heaven and new earth until we are perfect, until we are mature, until (to use a theological term) we are sanctified. Then we will be fit to go into that new universe without spoiling it.

If God took me into the new heaven and new earth as I am now I would spoil it very quickly – I would spoil it for myself, for you, for everybody else, and for him. So he is saving us. He has started us off on the road that leads to perfection. God wants us mature, wants us perfect, wants us completely restored to the image of God; he wants us to be the people he meant us to be when he first made us. When he has done that he is creating a new heaven and a new earth. One thing he says that is on almost the last page of our New Testament is: "Behold, I am making all things new." He has begun with us, but he will not stop until he has made the earth and the whole of space brand new for us to live in. That is why he is saving you.

3
HEARERS AND DOERS

Read James 1:19–27

A. RECEPTION OF THE WORD (19-21)
    1. Mental attitude (19)
        a. Quick to listen
        b. Slow to speak
        c. Slow to anger
    2. Moral attitude (20-21)
        a. Get rid of filth
        b. Get rid of prevalent evil
        c. Humbly accept

B. RESPONSE TO THE WORD (22-25)
    1. Forgetting (22-24) –the man in the mirror
        a. Looks b. Forgets c. Deceived
    2. Remembering (25) – the law of liberty
        a. Looks b. Remembers
        c. Blessed

C. RELIGION OF THE WORD (26-27)
    1. Controlled towards self (26)
        a. Loose talk b. Deceived
    2. Compassionate towards others (27a)
        a. Widows and orphans
        b. Not Widowers
    3. Conformed towards God (27b)
        a. Dirty world
        b. Uncontaminated

There are two problems with scripture: one is when you don't understand it and the second is when you do. This passage is so obvious in its meaning you don't need me to explain it. Nevertheless, we'll go through it. It is easy to grasp but hard to live, and that is like much of scripture. The connection with the previous passage we studied I think is that every good gift is from above, from the generous Father of lights. That is just picking up one of his two good gifts. I mentioned one was your birth as a Christian that came about through the truth, what James calls "the word of truth". In this section we are learning how to respond to that word.

So the first thing to notice is in vv. 19–21, receiving the Word. The Word is no use to you until you receive it, and the way you receive it is very important. You read it with the right attitudes. He says, "Note this," and it could be translated: "You know this perfectly well." You need to come to God's Word with a right mental attitude and a right moral attitude. Both are qualifications to have the benefit of God's Word. You can read the Bible in many other ways. You can read it for literature or for history, and many people have read it for other reasons but with the wrong attitude in mind.

So we look first at the mental attitude: that you want to know the truth. That is the first requirement when you come to scripture. You read it because you want to learn, and the most teachable people are the best ones to share the Bible with. The trouble is that unlearning is harder than learning, I find. That means revising your opinions is hard. If you have thought one way for a long time, it is not easy to be challenged.

Now the Lord has given us two ears and one mouth so that we can be quick to listen and slow to speak. It is the first part of the mental attitude that is needed if you are going to get the most out of the Word of truth. Quick to listen – salvation comes through hearing, not through talking but through listening to the gospel as someone is giving it to you. Jesus, when he was talking about the kingdom of God, kept saying, "He that has ears to hear, let him hear," because you may have ears but you may never hear. It means really not only to hear but to *heed* God's Word, to listen in the right way. Seed needs good ground and the Word of truth is the seed of the kingdom. Only in some people does that seed find good ground that has been prepared to receive it.

In farming we used to spend weeks preparing the seed ground. Ploughing, disking, harrowing – we would use all kinds of instruments behind a tractor to prepare the ground to receive the seed so that it would go right in and germinate and grow. There are not enough real listeners to the gospel, people who will use their ears properly. So quick to listen and slow to speak.

The church has too few listeners and too many speakers in my opinion. Being one of them, I am confessing something there. Many people would be happy if in preaching there could be dialogue, objections, heckling. But that does not suit the Word of God, it is because people are quicker to speak than to listen. This is the first mention in the letter of the tongue. James uses an interesting word for it, meaning "restless". We all have restless tongues; we all love to speak and to air our own views rather than to listen. I have heard group discussion described as "pooling your ignorance". That is not a bad description of a discussion group. It is not usually in discussion that people are saved.

I hope you will some day read *The Pilgrim's Progress*. It is a brilliant fictional account of the Christian life. Many characters in that book are very interesting. One of them is Mr Talkative and his father is a Mr Say-well from Prating-row. All these names in *The Pilgrim's Progress* are very poignant. It is a book that you should read and ask which of the characters is you. Well, I am probably like Mr Talkative.

Generally speaking I am, as my wife will tell you!

Too many are slow to listen and quick to speak. The problem with being quick to speak is that you then become quick to argue and object. When you argue with someone you tend to become irritated, and irritation sooner or later becomes anger. That is why James continues: slow to anger. He points out that anger in humans rarely brings righteousness into a life because most of our human anger is at the wrong time, with the wrong person, for the wrong reason, and in the wrong way. Just think of when you were last angry – did those four things apply? Maybe you got frustrated at work so you came home and took it out on your spouse – wrong person but you were angry so you let it out. So for the wrong reason, the wrong way, at the wrong time for the wrong person, and that is human anger in a nutshell. Jesus' anger was in the right way, with the right people, at the right time and the right place. He was so angry that he cleaned up the temple of the money changers single-handed. He took a whip and whipped people out of the temple. He didn't whip the animals out; he whipped the people who were dealing in them.

Jesus' anger, rare though it was, was very effective because it was right anger. Most of our anger is not very effective because it is wrong. So being quick to listen, slow to speak and slow to anger is the mental attitude that you need to come to God's Word. But it is more than that. The right mental attitude is that you want to learn, and therefore you want to listen more than you want to speak, but the right moral attitude is that you are reading it to be clean. In a word, you want to be saved. Jesus did not come to save us from hell – that is a bonus thrown in – he came to save us from all our sins. That is what he came to save us from. It is the scriptures that can make you wise unto salvation. So this is the second qualification for a student of God's Word.

I had a friend years ago who always went to the bathroom and washed his hands before he read the Bible. He wanted to read it with clean hands and a pure heart. Now I am not recommending that, but it was a gesture that was very meaningful. He was saying to the Lord, "I want to be clean." Then he would open his Bible with clean hands to read it. It is the moral attitude that is even more important than the mental. First, that we get rid of filth. If you are going to read the Bible with a dirty mind you will find dirt in it – there is plenty.

I remember a talk I heard as a little boy from a minister who was addressing the children in the congregation. He said there is a difference between clean dirt and dirty dirt. He challenged us, "Do you know the difference?" He said, "Clean dirt is on the outside of you and can be washed away. Dirty dirt is on the inside and it is not easy to get it washed away." Do you realise that we use on average seventy litres of clean water per day? It is a huge amount and water is going to be a crisis in this century – it is becoming very scarce. We use most of that seventy litres not to drink or even to cook, but to wash. We wash our clothes, we wash our bodies, we wash our cars, because this is basically a dirty world and people can't go through it without picking up dirt. Dirt is the natural form of existence, cleanliness is not, so we wash frequently. But if you are going to come and get benefit from the Bible you need an inner wash first. Get rid of all moral filth.

I remember the call of Isaiah when he said, "Lord, I'm a man of unclean lips." And notice: "Because I dwell in the midst of a people of unclean lips." He said an angel flew with a live coal from the altar and touched his lips, and the prophet Isaiah preached with a scarred mouth for the rest of his life. He would never forget that. Think of people looking at him and saying, "I wonder what happened to his mouth."

God cauterised it, cleaned him up, for he wanted to use Isaiah as his spokesman, but could not use a man with unclean lips to preach his word so needed to do that first.

It is an amazing call of God to a prophet. Get rid of moral filth. I should have put A and B together because it is virtually the same thing, but James uses another word: "prevalent" – "The evil that is so prevalent...." I don't need to underline that. Evil is everywhere in our world and it is impossible to walk through it without being aware of that. I am afraid it is difficult to walk through it and not pick it up. So you are contaminated from the world around you, you have been polluted, dirtied, and of course, Jesus was constantly casting out dirty spirits and pleading with us to allow the clean spirit, the Holy Spirit, to take their place.

Then he adds something else from moral attitude: if you are going to get benefit from reading the Bible you need to read it not proudly, but humbly, meekly, ready to submit to it, ready to allow it to speak to you, not judging the Word but being judged by it. You can go and listen to a preacher to judge the preacher, and that is a big mistake. You should go ready to hear the Lord speak to you through the Word, to be judged by – and humbly accept – God's Word.

These, then, are the two main conditions for receiving the Word of God and coming to it with the right attitude: the right mental attitude, and the right moral attitude. Then you can expect the Word to save you and to go on saving you, because then it can operate. So many people have a Bible at home on a shelf but it does them no good because they don't read it. Even those who read it don't always benefit because they are not coming to it with the right attitudes.

Now let us consider the response to the Word. It is not enough to receive it humbly and to receive it in the attitude we have been talking about, it is important to move on to responding to it. I think of all the many sermons I have heard in my life. How did I respond to them? Most of them I forgot within a few days. The next part of James talks about the sin of forgetting God's Word, forgetting what you have heard. So he talks about the reception first and then the response to God's Word. It involves first remembering it.

However often my wife listens to me, she always writes notes but she always gets something new. The only thing is that she sometimes quotes it back to me at the most inappropriate moment and expects me to live it. But I think it is an ideal partnership: I preach it, she lives it! Well, that's the little arrangement we have. Not quite! But James writes about forgetting – about a man who looks in a mirror, then walks away and within minutes has forgotten what he saw. For the Word of God acts like a mirror, you read about yourself.

I remember when we read the Bible right through in church at Guildford in Surrey. The mayor was a little man called Alderman Sparrow, an appropriate surname. A lapsed Roman Catholic, he heard we were reading the Bible right through, fifteen minutes at a time being read by each person, and he said, "Could I come and read? I'd like to, as Mayor of Guildford." We said yes, but the only space left was on Tuesday afternoon at 3.30. He said, "Yes, I can make that, and I'll bring my wife too. Would you mind if I wore a gold chain of office as mayor?" My colleague replied, "Well, not as long as you wear something else with it."

Sure enough, at 3.30 on the Tuesday afternoon, Alderman Sparrow turned up to read, and no wife. I said, "Where's your wife? You said you'd bring her."

"Oh, we've got unexpected visitors today. She had to get up at dawn and start cooking, making the beds and cleaning the house. She's just too busy and she sends her apologies. Now, what do I read?"

I said, "Well I don't know, you just get up at 3.30, take the

Bible, and read on from where the previous person stopped."

He read Proverbs 31! So he found himself reading about the perfect wife who gets up at dawn to cook for the family, clean the house, and all the rest of it. Then he read this, "Her husband is well known for he sits in the council chamber with the other civic leaders," and he started to smile, and he came back and sat by me. He said, "I've just been reading about myself in the Bible."

I said, "Most people find that happens when they read the Bible properly."

Then he bought a copy of the Bible and took it home to read to his wife.

As one old lady said, "Every message in the Bible has my name and address on it." That does happen. You look in a mirror and you see yourself. You read the Word of God and you see yourself, if you have got the right attitudes. But then that is not good enough if you go away and forget it.

Now I will confess something to you. Two days before giving the teaching in this chapter as a talk I was shaving and looking in the mirror, and I thought, "I need a haircut." Later that same day my wife said, "You need a haircut." I was so busy preparing for the event that it went right out of my mind and I still needed a haircut when the time came!

Do you see what happens? You look in a mirror, you see something that needs doing and you forget it. If you are too busy doing other things you forget what you have seen. Now a person like that will get nothing out of the Bible. They might get an occasional twinge of conscience, but it will still be forgotten if life is busy and there are other things to do. James is teaching that is what some people do with the Word of truth. They read it and they see themselves in it and they go away and forget it. Now he uses two words in the Greek for "look" that I can only translate as "glance" and "gaze". "The man that glances in a mirror is more likely to forget what he's seen than someone who gazes into a mirror intently looking for anything that needs doing."

Why do you have a mirror in your house? The point is to look into it and see that something is wrong with you and that you will have to do something about it. I shave every morning looking in the mirror. I use it to see myself and to see where I have not been and need to be. So that is the point of the Word. That is more than receiving the Word, that is really remembering. So the person who forgets will be deceived and get a wrong impression of themselves. They have had a glimpse of themselves in a mirror, they have seen something in the Word of God that has challenged them, and then they have forgotten it. Then they go away and then think they are as good as anybody else or that there is nothing to be put right or that they are really a perfect person. How easy it is to think of yourself as not needing any correction or anything putting right. It leads to deception.

The worst kind of deception is to deceive yourself. It is bad enough being deceived by other people, but when you forget what you have seen in the Word of God about yourself you are deceiving yourself and living in cloud cuckoo land, you are living in falsehood, in illusion. Whereas the person who gazes into the mirror and remembers to do something about what they have seen will be blessed. That is the simple alternative that James writes about: you glance in the Bible and forget what you saw, and you are deceived; or you gaze into the Bible, which means looking intently into it, studying it as if your life depends on it, and then you do something about it. You don't forget it, you go away and you do something, you will be blessed while you do it. In summary, if you want to be blessed by God, there is the recipe, which is very simple. Read his Word, remember it, do it and you will be blessed. That is a promise.

So much for the response to the Word. Let us move on to

the "Religion of the Word" as I have called it. What sort of person does God intend you to be? Why has he given you his Word? Why does he want you to read it, study it and look intently into it? Because it will help to make you the kind of person that he wanted you to be.

I guess that God is disappointed with us because he alone knows what we could have been by now if we had followed him perfectly. Let's look at the kind of person he wants you to be. What is his objective? So many people come to me and say, "I'm not religious." What do they mean by that? They often mean they don't go to church, they don't read their Bible, they don't pray, and a whole lot of other things.

James is concerned not with those people but with those who think they are religious. Of course many Jews do, and Jews in the Dispersion thought they were religious. Jews, even when they are scattered among the nations, usually practise circumcision with their children, their boys. They usually practise kosher kitchen, virtually having two kitchens, one for dairy products and one for meat and meat products. They usually keep the Sabbath more or less. If they can, they go to Jerusalem for the big three feasts of the year: Passover, Pentecost, and Tabernacles.

That is about the sum of it, so most Jews are religious to that extent. It is all outward and it is all "religious". But that is nothing like true religion. I know a lot of Christians who say, "I'm not religious, I'm a Christian," and I know what they mean. But here is the use of the word "religion" in your Bible: this is true religion, pure religion, and it is not a lot of church-going, it is something else. There are three dimensions to true religion in James's sight. Now James is against all sham, all unreality, he can't stand it. Jesus himself couldn't, calling it hypocrisy.

So here we have James' definition of the kind of religion that God wants. I am going to extract a principle from each example. The first example of true religion is someone who can have a tight rein on their tongue. In fact, later in this Epistle, James is going to say, "If anyone never says the wrong thing they must be perfect." It is a very good acid test of how perfect you are. If you never say the wrong thing you are perfect. Well that finds me out straight away. I identify with Peter in the Bible – he was always opening his mouth and putting his foot in it. The principle behind it is this: a truly religious person has total control over themselves, and therefore over their tongue, which is the hardest part of ourselves to control. So the first essence of true religion is to be in total self-control. It is interesting that the final fruit of the Spirit in Galatians 5 is self-control. That is a mark of a truly religious person. They have total control over themselves and therefore over their tongue. If you are able to control your tongue you can control everything else.

Loose talk is dangerous. Jesus himself said, "For every careless word we shall be brought into judgement." A careless word is what you say when you are not in control and somehow things slip out that you never intended to say, and afterwards wish you hadn't said. It is in what Jesus called our "idle words" that we often reveal our true selves. So that is the first thing in true religion: control of self, no loose talk, or, James says, you are deceiving yourself. If you are not controlling your tongue and you think you are religious you are in illusion, deceiving yourself, which as I have pointed out is the worst kind of deception, the most difficult to detect and the most difficult to cure.

The second mark of true religion is to visit widows and orphans in their distress. What is their distress? Their distress is that they have lost a husband or a father. Those are very distressing occasions. They were even more so in the ancient world where there was little hope for widows or orphans. They had lost the man of the family. Did you ever notice that the people raised from the dead were sons of widows? Because a widow in her distress was left without her man. In the Bible, which is everywhere a paternal or patriarchal society, the father was the important one to be the provider and the protector of his wife and children. In the modern egalitarian thinking or liberal thinking of today, men and women are equal, meaning the same, having the same role and responsibility. Not so in the Bible. In the Bible the responsibility of the man is to protect his wife and provide for her and to protect the children and provide for them. In fact, it says in my New Testament that if a man does not provide for his own family he is worse than an unbeliever. That is a devastating indictment, isn't it? So widows and orphans are to be cared for. The principle behind that is the principle of compassion for those who cannot look after themselves. That is a mark of true religion. It has been, wonderfully, and still is.

I think of George Müller, the classic example. If you go to Bristol today you can still see the big building up on the hill where he housed hundreds of orphans because they had no father. He became a father to hundreds. There were times that his faith was really stretched. One of them was when they all sat down for breakfast and there was no food. They had not got any. George Müller got up and said grace and thanked God for the food he was supplying. Empty plates, empty tables, and he thanked God for the food! At that point a baker's van broke down outside the orphanage and its wheel came off. They could not do anything with all the bread in the van so they gave it to George Müller and he carried it in and they all fed. A great man. I wish people knew George Müller for his teaching as well as his work among the orphans because his teaching is magnificent. I would have been a follower of his if I had been alive, and I have preached in his Brethren Assembly in Bristol. He was a great teacher, a German, who came over here.

Dr. Barnardo was another Christian who showed his care for orphans. Still to this day there are Christians in England who go abroad, taking money and clothes to give to orphans. There is a long record of Christians who had real religion, pure and honest religion, and had compassion for those who could not provide for themselves.

Why then no widowers? Did you notice that? God himself describes himself in the book of Psalms five times as, "I will be a father to the fatherless and a husband to the widow." But he doesn't seem to care for widowers. Of course statistically husbands are likely to die before their wives, so there are far more widows than widowers. "But God, don't you care about widowers?" Yes of course he does, but he regarded the men as responsible for the provision and protection of families. That is why he just mentions widows and orphans. They are those who find it difficult to provide for themselves. Today I think he would talk about single mothers because they are in among the most difficult situations where men have walked out on them and left them with children and no provision. That is where this kind of compassion would show. We had in our church an elder who was responsible for the widows in the church and he did a superb job. Since he was a builder he replaced broken panes of glass in windows, repaired fuses, all sorts of things, and he really served widows.

The church has always had a concern for widows. Paul in his letter to Timothy was very practical. He said that older widows need you more because younger widows have a chance of marrying again. So right through two thousand years of Christian history there has been a concern for widows and orphans which has shown itself. The principle behind it is the principle of compassion for other people, and especially those who cannot look after themselves.

The third thing about pure religion is to keep yourself

uncontaminated by the world. But it means unpolluted –
"unspotted" is the old translation. Again I underline that
James faces up to the fact that this is a dirty world and as
you go through it you can be contaminated, polluted, without
realising it. You just become part of the world. The word
"world" in our New Testament is always a bad word. It is a
word that means "our sinful society", the sum of that society
and all the people in it.

We have to face the facts, it is a sinful world, a dirty world,
and it is not easy to walk through it uncontaminated. Now the
principle here is that as God's people you want to conform
to God. In the Old Testament and the New, God says, "Be
holy because I am holy." He has chosen us to be his people
and that involves being like him, and he is not contaminated
by the world at all.

From John 3:16 we know that God loved the world, but
the same author writes in his letter: "Do not love the world".
So God did so, but he told us not to. John goes on, "... or
anything in the world. If anyone loves the world, the love
of the Father is not in him." At first sight it seems to be a
contradiction that God loved the world but we are not to do
so. There is a reason why he did. The reason is that he was
not contaminated by it; it was not a source of temptation
to him because he is holy. In a sense it was safe for God to
love the world, but it is not safe for us. That is what John
is teaching.

Now that is not saying we should not love the people in
it, but the world as a system is not God's world. It is a fallen
world, a world that is in trouble, and the Bible explains how
it got into trouble and how it will ever get out of it. But here
is this word "world". Some Christians have interpreted this in
a rather naïve way concerning external things: that Christians
should not dance, should not wear makeup, should not do
this, should not do that. No, worldliness is much more subtle

than that, and therefore much more difficult to spot and to deal with. It is to think like other people. It is to want what they want. It is to be just like them. We are called to be in the world, not to get out of the world – we are to be in it but not of it. It was only safe for God to love the world as he did. It is not safe for us. The system into which we were born, which we have been part of, we have got out of now, hopefully. We may not have got entirely out of it, and it takes a lifetime to realise how much of the world is still in us. But he set us on what he calls "the way" of salvation.

I am not saved yet, I am looking forward to being saved – aren't you? I get silence when I say that to believers. Is it a new thought to you? Well let me remind you of some of the verses in scripture. In Romans, Paul says, "We are nearer our salvation than when we first believed." Now too many people look back to the time they first believed and say, "That's when I was saved." But the New Testament teaches us to look forward to our complete salvation from every sin there is in us. So I am looking forward to that. Only then will I get a new body, a new outside as well as a new inside. I can't wait to get it because it's a body just like his risen ascended body, therefore I will be thirty-three years old. That really appeals to me!

"Be holy as I am holy." One of the most amazing things that God ever said is: "Your sins will be whiter than snow." Have you ever had the embarrassing experience of hanging up washing after there has been a snowfall and you had thought you had got your clothes clean, and they look filthy compared with the pure white snow? That is what Jesus wants us to be – like pure white snow; a person who shares that will keep themselves untainted from the world, uncontaminated.

Now there is true religion. Notice that it takes all three of those principles to make it, not just one or two. There are plenty of people who like one principle, especially the middle one there, compassion for the needy, and they feel that is all of Christianity and all that religion requires. No, it requires self-control and conforming to God's holiness. We need all three and if there is anything the world needs, it is that – all three in balance.

I believe that in this section of his letter James is very like the Old Testament prophets. They would not stand for anything less than pure religion. They would always criticise the absence of any of these three things.

4
FAVOURITISM AND FREEDOM

Read James 2:1–13

A. SOCIAL FAVOURITISM (1-4)
    1. Partiality (1-3)
        a. Rich seated
        b. Poor stand or sit on floor
    2. Damnation (4)
        a. Judges b. Evil thoughts

B. SUPERFICIAL FALLACY (5-7)
    1. Insulting the (rich) poor
        a. Chosen by God
        b. Rich in faith
        c. Heirs of Kingdom
    2. Indulging the (poor) rich
        a. Exploiting b. Suing
        c. Slandering

C. SERIOUS FELONY (8-11)
    1. Keeping the Law (8)
        a. Royal law b. Doing right
    2. Breaking the law (9-11)
        a. Part b. Whole

D. SEVERE FATE (12-13)
    1. Human judgement – with mercy (12)
        a. Going to be judged
        b. By law of liberty
    2. Divine judgement – without mercy (13)
        a. Not been merciful
        b. Triumph over judgement

There are two key words in James that sum up the whole letter: "Do" and "Don't". Now we come to the first "Don't". It is a very simple one: "Do not try to combine faith in our glorious Lord Jesus Christ with favouritism." The two do not belong together, they are contradictory. Faith comes from the Word, favouritism comes from the world, and to try and combine them is a very big mistake. More than that, it is a sin.

That is the main "Don't" of the first part of chapter 2. This is the first of four passages in the letter against rich people and you wonder if he has become biased. But let us look a little deeper at what he says. First, remember this is a letter from a Messianic Jew in Jerusalem to all the Messianic Jews in the Diaspora around the world. Many Jews had left the Promised Land and gone to live elsewhere in the Roman Empire. It was now easy to travel. There were good roads; there was security, the Roman peace. They were getting wealthier and they had left for one reason and one reason only – trade and business. They had gone to make money, and they had scattered around the Roman Empire, trading, which Jews have done ever since. This time this led to a great gap between the rich and the poor, because when you are in a free-for-all mercantile society, when you are free to trade and free to do business, some get very rich and others get very poor.

This is happening in our own society right now, as the gap between rich and poor is getting bigger. It does in a free trade area. Those who are clever at trade make money and those who are not lose it. In fact, it is worse than that because the rich exploit the poor to make their money. That is why, for example, some bank directors today are more concerned with lining their own pockets and retiring with a big bonus than serving their own customers.

Among the dispersed Jews to a great degree there were some who were exceptionally rich and many who were quite poor. It is interesting that evangelism in that situation usually appeals more to the poor than the rich. The rich have enough money to meet all their needs. The poor do not, and they therefore are more responsive to a gospel of help by the divine grace. So most of the dispersed Jews who became believers in the Messiah (and therefore what we call Messianic Jews) were from the poor end of the social scale.

That is the background to the letter and it explains a great deal of James's apparent prejudice against the rich and for the poor. What is the connection in his mind with the previous passage? The answer is that he says pure religion requires keeping oneself unspotted or untainted by the world. This first half of chapter 2 is an example of how even Christians can get spotted by the world, tainted and corrupted, and begin to reflect worldly standards instead of Word standards.

So James begins with this big "don't": "Don't combine faith and favouritism." That is combining salvation and sin in one go. They are incompatible. This is pollution by the world, and it can happen in a church as it happened among those Messianic believers. Partiality is a sin of corporate behaviour. He wants us to imagine this scene: two visitors come into your fellowship. He calls them a synagogue, but that word is simply "come together"; it is a lovely word, focusing not on the building but on the people. Indeed, the word "church" does the same. In the Greek it is the word *ekklesia*, meaning "out of", "called". So the church in the Greek means "the called out". It is virtually the same as the synagogue – "come together", a gathering of people in God's name. The two new people, who have not been to your fellowship before, come in and immediately you do something wrong. You look at the outside, you jump to conclusions (which is the only exercise some people get!), and you have decided already which one you want in the fellowship. If you can get that rich man in the fellowship that is really going to help the church – do you see what I mean? That is judging entirely by first impression and outside visibility. One man has good clothes and is wearing gold rings, so when you see that in the ancient world you immediately think that man is rich. Then you look at the other man who came in with him and he is in shabby clothes. To treat one man differently from the other is so easy to do.

Notice the difference between the two words "here" and "there". They say to the rich man, "Sit here," and to the shabby man, "Go there." It is a here and there situation, and "here" is a good comfortable seat at the front where they can see everything and "there" is either to stand at the back or sit on the floor. In just saying "here" to the one and "there" to the other you have sinned. You have shown that you are influenced by the world and not by the Word of God. You are now polluted by the world and you have polluted the fellowship. He says: "You have done it among yourselves." If that is your attitude to the outsider it will also be your attitude to the insider, and that is going to spoil the fellowship because it means that you will pay more attention to the rich members and less attention to the poor members. It is so easy to judge by the outside, by the appearance of someone. It is so easy to assume that if someone is wealthy they have been successful and therefore they must be important. That is the kind of thinking that goes on.

Partiality is a complete contradiction of our belief in God. We will see that it is not the way God treats people, but it is the way we can treat them so easily, and it is a terrible mistake. What we say to people when they arrive reveals our attitude towards them and it comes out of our mouth, as most sins do, as Jesus taught us. The words spoken come from the heart and they come out of your mouth and they reveal what you really think about others.

What is wrong with all this? The first thing is in v. 4: "You are guilty of prejudice." That word means to pre-judge, to decide quickly beforehand, and you have set yourself up as judges with evil thoughts. That is a strong word, "evil", yet it is the word that James uses. There is nothing more offensive to people than a judge who is partial. In any court of law if the public suspect that the judge is partial to some people and not to others it is a scandal and it finds its way into the newspapers usually. A judge who has decided beforehand how to judge people there would not be a true judge – there would be a miscarriage of justice, something terribly wrong. James says, "You have become judges with evil thoughts," and any court of law where that happened could or should be condemned widely, especially if the deciding factor in the judge's mind is money. If a wealthy person were to get off a traffic offence because they are wealthy then there would be an outcry straight away. If a celebrity were to get away with wrongdoing, the judge would be blamed very quickly and publicly. That is what James is saying to people who do this kind of thing: you are setting yourself up as judges and you have prejudices, you have pre-judged the situation and therefore you have already committed a miscarriage of justice. But in this case there is not only human justice but divine justice – you have gone right against how God thinks and feels about people, and that is a serious offence.

James is going to go on building up this case bit by bit to show how terribly serious it is. So we are going to move on to the next thing. He is saying: you have made a very big mistake in this prejudice that you have shown. It reveals shallow, even silly thinking.

Now he takes the whole situation to a deeper level. He is going to criticise his readers very heavily but he begins by saying, "My dear brothers," which is a tactful way to begin. He points out that he is a Christian and they are Christians and he is appealing to their Christian conscience. But he says,

"Do you realise that you've first of all insulted the poor?"
And in God's eyes that is a very serious thing to do. You
have insulted the poor because they are poor and that reveals
this deep prejudice. You can't flatter a rich man without
insulting a poor man, the two things go together; they are
two sides of the same coin. He says, "You've insulted the
rich poor man." I put that in to show the kind of paradox that
there is in the next few verses. He said, "You're insulting
the poor who are rich." Then he is going to say, "And you
are indulging the rich who are poor." It is a very interesting
re-judgement of the situation. You are actually insulting the
really rich people in insulting the poor. How is that? First
because God chooses mostly poor people. He does choose
some rich, but as Paul says in Corinthians, "Not many noble
are called." It is the nobodies that God likes and he turns
them into somebodies. That is a lovely note sounded in
scripture. It is true of the whole Bible. God chose the Jews.
There is a little poem: "How odd of God to choose the Jews,
but odder still for those who choose the Jewish God and
scorn the Jews." But God chose the poor. When he chose
the Jewish nation for his own, to be his chosen people, they
were slaves in Egypt, they had nothing. They had no money
of their own, no name of their own, no weapons of their own.
God chose them precisely for that reason. Egypt was a great
nation. They built the pyramids, they had pharaohs, but God
did not choose them. He chose the nation that had nothing
because that is the way God thinks. He chooses nobodies
and he makes them into somebodies. We can see that in any
church congregation. God has chosen the poor.

Secondly, he has chosen them not because they are poor
but because they are rich in faith. That is the true measure of
someone's wealth. A person who is rich in faith is wealthy,
and that is God's outlook and the church's outlook, or it
should be. Yet in this welcoming the rich man and the poor

man, they didn't even stop to think if either of them had faith. They just immediately assumed that a successful man financially is an important man in God's sight. I am afraid there are some Christians who think that way and are very glad when a lot of rich people join their church, because that ensures the church's future, which is a terrible mistake.

But there is a third reason: when God chooses someone in Christ he makes them an heir. Not just a son, but a son and heir, and therefore they are going to inherit the world one day. Who is rich? The rich man is going to lose everything he has got one day and it won't be too long ahead. A shroud has no pocket. The rich man is going to be a very poor man, but the poor man is going to be a very rich man. He has a huge legacy coming to him, he is wealthy in God's sight already. That is why I said that one of the mistakes is that you are insulting the "rich poor man". You have got it all wrong. He is very rich and his riches will last and he will inherit everything, all things are his in Christ.

Do you ever think of yourself as an heir as well as a son or daughter of God? You are an inheritor, you have something big coming to you. That is the Christian's outlook. How much are you worth? Well, I am worth the whole world – it is all mine in Christ. I am Christ's and he has made me an heir, to inherit all creation. What a silly mistake we have made in showing flattery to the wealthy man who came in. Now we have not only insulted the rich poor man, we have indulged the poor rich man.

We don't stop to ask how he made his wealth. The answer is that he made it in a competitive trading world. You cannot be in that and not get caught up in other things too unless you are a very strong Christian. A Christian businessman can maintain his character under all the pressures, and it is done, but it is a miracle. It is even hard for a man who is rich to enter the kingdom. Jesus said that. It is hard for such a person to realise his real need as a sinner, which is desperate. Not impossible though – Jesus said all things are possible with God and it does happen, and we can thank God that it does. But we should never fall into the trap of thinking anybody who is rich is successful and has "made it", as we say.

How did this rich man get his wealth? James is going to assume some pretty bad things. He has got rich by his treatment of the poor. Therefore that must have been pretty normal in James' day. A rich man who has made his money without dealing badly with the poor was almost unknown. He may have made his money by exploiting others, by driving hard bargains; in so many ways he is an exploiter, an oppressor. By and large it is true in our world that the rich oppress the poor, and that is how they make their money. Trading becomes a jungle, a highly competitive business in which you can't make a fortune without other people losing a great deal.

I think, for example, of what is called "money trading" in our world, the banks supporting people who make their money by moving money around the world, keeping their eyes glued to the computer screen to watch where the rises and falls are occurring. If you make money in that world you are doing it at the loss of other people, it is gambling. One of the roots of gambling, or one of the definitions of gambling, is gaining at someone else's loss. If you gamble and win something lots of people have lost, you cannot make huge sums of money without somebody else losing it. I mean unreasonable profits, big profits usually built on other people's loss.

Not only that, but being rich they can afford lawyers and therefore they drag you to court. Litigation becomes almost the hobby of unfair traders. They drag you to courts for their own ends. They can afford to do so. They can fight your wages, they can claim your debts, they can up your rents, and they can do it all legally. So not only do they exploit you, and there were no industry regulators in those days, the rich could drive hard bargains and take advantage of need in the market by upping prices unnecessarily. "The rich slander the name by which you are called."

James is making sweeping statements but it does sound as if it was the general situation in his day among the dispersed Messianic Jews. He would not have said all these things unless it was common. Bear in mind that James, the head of the Jerusalem church, was the fairest man that we know of in the New Testament. He was called "James the Just". So he would not have said all this unless there was truth in it. But they were slandering the noble name by which the Christians were called; they were those who were misusing the name of Jesus Christ – maybe as a swear word. That can happen, and it obviously was happening. These were very serious charges, but did not apply to *all* rich or *all* poor. It is a generalisation and there are some exceptions. There are some people who are poor and are not rich in faith, and there are some rich people who are rich in faith as well. So let us not take what is a generalisation and make it a universal condemnation.

Favouritism, involving misjudging rich and poor is a big mistake, it could be a miscarriage of justice and a serious felony. For the first time, James introduces this concept that favouritism is breaking the law – not human law but the law of God. That is a serious charge.

At first sight this paragraph looks like a complete change of subject, but it is not because the word "favouritism" is still there in it. He is still thinking about this situation and as if it is not serious enough already he takes it to a deeper level still. He says this is a sin because it is breaking God's law. Now he begins this paragraph with an unusual word about the royal law of loving your neighbour, saying: if you are keeping the royal law of loving your neighbour, that is fine, you are doing well. Why should he say that? Well, I have missed out a very important little word in the original Greek which means "really", "truly". It makes this into a question. If you are really obeying the royal law, love your neighbour as yourself, well and good – why does James write that? Most commentators say (and I agree), they were using the law (love your neighbour) to justify the way they were treating the rich person. They were using the law as an excuse. They said: we are supposed to love our neighbour and all we are doing in giving that rich man a good seat in the synagogue is loving our neighbour as ourselves – what's wrong with that? They seem to have been blind to what they had done to the man in shabby clothes and to have forgotten him altogether. They were justifying their flattery. So James was saying: if that is really what you are doing, if that is truly the reason you do it, that is well and good, but I want to remind you that the law of God is a whole law and if you break any part of it you have broken all of it.

That is not the way we usually think, yet in a sense it is. If I am stopped for speeding on the motorway and the policeman says to me, "You've broken the law", and I say to him, "But look, I've just come out of town and I stopped at every red light and I kept to 30 m.p.h. in the town," he will laugh at me because I am using one part of the law to cancel another. The law is a whole law. He will still say, "You've broken the law." So in our popular speech we regard the law as a whole thing. In other words, if you break the law at any point you have become a lawbreaker and you are no longer a law keeper. God's law, as distinct from human laws, is all of one piece – many parts, but all the parts make up a whole. This is the way God tells us to live, and if we break it at any point we have broken it all. It is like a pearl necklace, and if you break it at any point the pearls are lost, the wholeness has been lost. When justifying their special attention to the rich man because of loving our neighbour, which they were supposed to do, they were neglecting many of the other laws of God.

James then used a fairly obvious illustration. The law of God says don't kill – don't murder – and don't commit adultery. It is no use saying "Well, I've done one but not the other", because it doesn't cancel things out. You can keep part of the law but that doesn't cancel out what you've broken, you have become a lawbreaker.

Just to bring a little of my sense of humour here, there is a pastor in London, pastor of the London Healing Mission whose name is Roy Jeremiah, unusual name, but there it is. There is an American evangelist living in Singapore called the Reverend John Haggai. Roy Jeremiah invited John Haggai to come and preach at the London Healing Mission. On the Sunday morning they set off in Roy Jeremiah's car to go to the church and they were late so they broke the speed limit and were travelling about forty-five into London. But it was Sunday morning and there was very little traffic. But there was a policeman on duty and he stopped the car. He said to the driver, "And what's your name?" He said, "Jeremiah." The policeman smiled a bit and turned to the passenger, "And what's your name?" He said, "Haggai." So the policeman said, "Well my name's Moses and you just broke my law." That will help you to remember the point.

To break just one part of God's law is to become a person who is not living God's way and not doing God's will. Whether it is a little law or a big one, it is part of a whole picture. This is the way God wanted us to be as a whole. Did you know that in the Old Testament there are 613 laws? To break one of them is to become a lawbreaker. But those 613 laws were given to Jews as their national constitution. Do you know how many imperatives there are in the New

Testament – the do's and don'ts in the New Testament? There are actually over 1100. We have twice as many laws to live by. The law of Christ is not easier to keep; it is harder to keep than that of Moses. We often forget that Christians, whilst not under the law of Moses, are under the law of Christ. If you question that, check me out. Go through your New Testament making a list of all the do's and the don'ts. We have nearly twice as many as the Jews had. To break one of those is to stop living God's way. It is to become a lawbreaker. Therefore, if we pay attention to the rich and not to the poor, if we say "Here" to the rich and "There" to the poor, it is a very serious felony judged by God's law.

But that is not the end of it. You might think that James had said enough about this simple matter of the way we have invited two people into the fellowship, but he is going to take it even further. He says, "You're going to be judged." Every Christian knows this, and this brings a whole new dimension into practical matters of daily life. All of us are going to face the judgement, and the judgement of God is very clear.

Jesus said, "Blessed are the merciful for they shall obtain mercy." And notice it is the future: they *shall* obtain mercy. If you hope for mercy on the day of judgement then you had better be merciful now. If we don't show mercy now we shall be judged then without mercy at all. That is a very serious statement, "Blessed are the merciful for they shall obtain mercy." If we want any mercy from God in the day when we stand before him to render an account for our life then it is important that he is able to say, "You have been merciful and therefore I can be too." That is quite a thought, isn't it? That is the main thought here, that a severe fate is awaiting those who don't show mercy. For mercy and judgement are opposites. "Mercy triumphs over judgement," or to change the word slightly, "Mercy triumphs over justice." Justice gives us what we deserve. Mercy is to give us what we don't deserve and have no merit for at all. If we hope that God will treat us better than we deserve in the future than we had better treat others now better than they deserve. This final indictment of the situation in their synagogue is very serious indeed, because all of us will stand before the judgement seat, and therefore we had better think about this.

Is James making a mountain out of a molehill? After all, it was just a matter of welcoming two visitors to the fellowship. But no, he is declaring that this is very serious because it is being tainted by the world.

So let us apply this. First of all, it applies not just to the rich, but to rank. As a chaplain in the Royal Air Force, rank was a part of our life. Everybody was below somebody else or above somebody else. I heard from a chaplain about a service of Holy Communion in the Army. As often happens in the Church of England they filed out to receive the bread and the wine row by row. The last man out of a row in the congregation was a private soldier. As he stepped into the aisle he realised he was stepping in front of the first person in the row behind, who was a major. Instinctively he stepped back and let the major go first, but thankfully the major did not go first and he beckoned to the man: "You first." Then he said this, "Everywhere else you'd be right, but not here." That major was a true Christian. He understood that in God's people rank doesn't matter and shouldn't matter. What a lovely thing.

Let's consider something else: celebrity. Cliff Richard started attending our church at Millmead. I remember the first time he came. He always came at the last minute for obvious reasons, so that he would not get flooded with attention. That is why very often he had to sit on the floor, because every seat was taken long before the last minute. If anybody came late they just had to sit on the steps in the auditorium. So he came in the first time and he sat on the floor. To my surprise, and indeed horror, somebody sitting in a pew near where he was on the floor immediately got up and offered him the seat. He didn't accept it, he stayed on the floor. That was the only time that happened. From then on, if he was late he sat on the floor like everybody else and was given no special treatment at all. When he came to us I said, "Cliff, I will never ask you to sing. If the Holy Spirit tells you to sing you are welcome to come out and do so, but here you are a brother and there will be no special treatment. You are one of us." He really appreciated being able to come to a place where he didn't get any special treatment. I think perhaps I ought to add that my wife had the problem to deal with girls from Australia or New Zealand who saved up for a single ticket to come and marry him. You would be amazed! She dealt with them very effectively. But the main thing was that a celebrity should not have special treatment in the house of God. Most of the congregation got the message fairly quickly.

Let us take something else – the question of ethnicity. Now funnily enough, there is a temptation the opposite way nowadays. I don't talk about black and white because there are only pink and brown, and God is "colour blind" anyway. But there was a day in English churches when, if a white man and a black man came in, the white man was shown to the seat and the black man was left to find his own place. We are now in the opposite position, where there is "positive discrimination" as it is called. There are "black churches" and they are tempted when a white person comes in to do the opposite and to give them special treatment. It is because in both cases it was a minority and the majority was exercising prejudice. Thank God that is going. I hope soon it will be gone altogether. But it still happens in some fellowships.

Here is a big one: what would you do if a member of the royal family came to your church? That is where it really would be a test, especially if every seat was already taken.

Just ask yourself what you would do. The Queen, I really believe, is a believer in Jesus, a sister in Christ. I hope that is how she would be received in a fellowship. I am trying to give you just a feel of what James is tackling here. It is so easy to bring worldly attitudes and standards into a Christian fellowship where such things don't belong. We are trying then to combine faith and favouritism and they don't mix and they should never be found in any fellowship. So try to make your church one that has no special treatment for anybody, but welcomes all in the name of Christ.

5
FAITH AND WORKS (1)

Read James 2:14 –26

A. ASSUMPTION, ANALOGY and
   ASSERTION (14-17)
    1. Assumption –
    faith without works cannot save (14)
    2. Analogy –
    love without works cannot support (15-16)
    3. Assertion –
    faith without works cannot survive (17)
B. ARGUMENT and ANSWER (18-26)
    1. Argument – faith versus works (18-20a)
      a. You have faith and I have works
      b. You cannot demonstrate your faith
      c. Your faith is no better than demonic
    2. Answer – faith works (20b – 26)
      a. Contrast – good man Abraham,
              bad woman Rahab
      b. Comparison – both risked future
      c. Conclusion – inactive faith dead

This is the most controversial part of the Epistle. Some very strong statements here really upset Martin Luther, on the basis of which he called it "an epistle of straw". What he meant was that it had no nourishment in it, nothing to get his teeth into; he didn't feel it built him up at all. That was strong language, but Luther was hooked on the gospel, and he said there is no gospel in this letter. Therefore, for him, it should not have been in the New Testament. Indeed, as Professor of New Testament in Wittenburg University he forbade his students to study James.

We will come to that in the next chapter because this is such a controversial passage we will consider it in two ways, the first of which is exegetical – so in this chapter we are simply going to look at the passage and what it actually says. Then, in the following chapter, we will look at some theological aspects of the passage.

The connection with our study so far is at 2:1 where James is saying: don't try and hold the faith and favouritism. But now he explains what he means by holding the faith. Do his readers have a right understanding of what faith really is? So he is now discussing the matter of faith, and the overall message is that faith and action belong together.

The key word here is "deeds" or "works" – in Greek, *erga*. You may be familiar with the word "ergonomics", which is from the same word and it means *action*. In a new car you find that the ergonomics have been studied carefully, the movements of your arms and hands, where the switches are, and they have designed the layout so that you can easily reach the controls you need. They have even put the gear change and the radio switches on the steering wheel. They study the actions of the human body when driving a car, and they try to fit cars to driver actions.

So *erga* does not just means "deeds" it means "actions". In fact I think a lot of misunderstanding of this passage would have been avoided if the word "works" was not used in translations but rather the word "actions". James is teaching about faith that acts, faith that works, faith that is not passive but active – because the one thing he can't stand is sham religion, based on profession but not practice. The difference between faith that does not act and faith that does act is his real concern.

So, having given a preview of the conclusion, let us now see how he arrives at it. The real key question for any religion is this: how does that religion relate faith and works? Those are the two great subjects of religion, doctrine and duty. Christianity alone among all the world religions says faith comes first and then actions. That is the usual understanding. But James is saying something a little more than that and we have to realise what he is saying. The quickest way to analyse this section of his letter is to do so by examining the figures of speech, the arguments he uses.

Therefore in the first section (vv. 14–17) we look at three things. We look at an assumption he makes, an analogy he draws and then an assertion he makes. I have deliberately chosen those three words so that you see the difference between them. Let us look at the assumption. He makes this assumption by asking what are called rhetorical questions. That means asking a question when you hope that you will get the right answer. It usually means you do not want the answer given because it is assumed. He has these two rhetorical questions, both about faith without action, without works, without deeds.

The first question is: what good is it? He expects everybody to answer: "No good at all." The second question is: "Can such faith save him?" Again he expects a negative answer. Mind you, James is not entirely sure that he will get that answer, so he now uses an analogy to back that up. It is what Jesus was always doing with his parables: the kingdom of heaven is *like....* Basically, it is a parable. James says: "Now suppose that one of your fellow believers...." That is the meaning of "Suppose a sister or a brother...." He is now speaking about people within the fellowship. Suppose you meet a brother or sister who is starving and shivering, that he lacks enough food for the day and lacks enough clothing and you say to him.... James actually has the person saying:

"Bless you; God will supply your food and clothes that you need." We could think of a modern equivalent. "Goodbye" is short for "God be with ye" and originally was a typical religious expression used in daily life – "God be with ye." We use it in such a way that we don't realise we are talking about God. But this man is simply wishing them well. He is using words of comfort without any deeds of comfort. You just need to state that, and it is so obvious that it is a useless thing to do or say. You are not helping that person if you just say, "Well, God bless you and may God find you some food and clothes." It is no good.

Now I want to underline that this is an analogy. He is not here describing the works that he has mentioned before. He is not saying that faith without this kind of activity is useless. My proof is not just the word "suppose" but the word at the end of it. He says: "In the same way, faith without works is dead." The word translated here "In the same way" is a Greek word (οὕτως) which means "likewise". It means "so", "even so", "just so". It is underlining that this is purely a parable, a likeness. I mention that because this is where many people have gone wrong with James. They have assumed he is saying that faith without works of love is useless. He is not saying that at all.

He is saying, "*In the same way*, love without works is useless." Faith without works is useless, love without works is useless. It is an analogy, and therefore we are not to assume that it is part of his argument for works. He will later give us two illustrations of what he does mean, which are not works of love at all, they are works of faith. This is the first distinction I want you to get very clear in your mind: works of love and works of faith are two different things. But just as love without deeds is useless, so faith without deeds is useless. Have you got the picture? That word "likewise" or translated in the New International Version as "In the same way". By the way, that is the same Greek word "so" in John 3:16, which is so misunderstood. It does not mean God "sooo" loved the world, meaning "so much" or "so deeply". It means "in the same way" God loved the world. That drives you back to vv. 3:14–15 to understand what 3:16 means. Read my little book on John 3:16. Most people misunderstand that verse completely by interpreting "so" to mean "*sooo* much", "*sooo* deeply". "As Moses lifted up the serpent in the wilderness, even so [οὕτως; in the same way] he will lift up the Son of Man." We should not really say, "For God 'so' loved the world...." We should say, "For in the same way, God loved the world...."

Back then to James 2:17. James is illustrating a principle, but he is not illustrating what he means by works of faith. He is saying, as in the case of love and sympathy, if you do not give the person the necessities of life it is useless. You are not helping them by saying, "God bless you, brother." Often we can use that phrase "God bless you" to avoid doing anything about someone's need. The principle is that without deeds love can be useless, and therefore without deeds faith can be useless. But it is not the same kind of deeds, and that is the point I want to make very strongly.

So having made an assumption in asking two questions and having backed that up with a parable or a metaphor or a simile, James is saying: now you understand what I am saying, I can make a straight statement, an assertion. He makes the assertion that faith without works cannot survive. It is dead, it has no life in it, and therefore it cannot help. Many have missed that key phrase "In the same way". He is not talking about the works of love now. He is back to talking about the fact that faith without action is dead in itself. I want you to notice that faith and works go together. It is not that faith must lead to works, it is that faith must have works, it must *act*.

Or, to put it very simply, faith is not something you think, it is not something you feel, it is not even something you say. It is something you *do*, and that applies to repentance also. It is not just feeling sorry or even saying sorry, it is being sorry enough to do something. Or as a schoolboy defined repentance: "It's being sorry enough to stop." I think that is as good a definition of repentance as I have ever come across. So he is saying now, categorically: faith that doesn't act doesn't save. If you don't do anything with your faith it can't do anything for you – a very strong statement. But we are going to explore that further.

Now James moves on to an argument, and the answer to that argument. I have to confess at this point I get lost – the next few verses I really don't fully understand. He is now imagining a heckler, an objector, someone joining in and objecting to his straight statement that faith without works is dead. It is an interesting objection. Do bear in mind that James is imagining what the heckler will say. But I think he must have had this kind of objection frequently when he preached, and that there were people who came to him afterwards and said, "I don't agree with you," or, "Did you really mean this?" – as every preacher gets. So he is basing it on real objections.

Paul did this in Romans 6. He said, "Shall we say, 'Let's sin that grace may abound'?" An extraordinary thing – and Paul is imagining an objector saying that. That must be because he has had that objection. Therefore he puts the imaginary conversation into Romans just as James is putting this imaginary conversation into his letter. Now the problem arises, and I am sorry if this raises problems with you that you never knew existed, leading to confusion – but you need to be aware – there are differences of opinion about what James means. The other problem we have is not imagination, but punctuation, because the original Greek New Testament had no punctuation marks in it. They simply wrote the Greek letters in one long string of letters with no quotation marks, no commas, no full stops, nothing. So you have sometimes got to imagine where the punctuation would come. In the next few verses in the original manuscript we don't have the punctuation. What difference does that make? Quite simply, we do not know where the objection ends.

If you look at the NIV you find the inverted commas come immediately after the first sentence in this little section, and therefore you assume that the rest of this paragraph is James's reply. But the more I have looked into it the more I cannot fit that in. I just don't understand what James is trying to say if he is making those two comments. Let us look at the three comments and what they say first, and then begin to ask who is saying it.

The first comment is: "You have faith and I have works." I am quite sure that is the objector talking. Then the NIV closes the quotation marks. The second statement is: "You can't demonstrate your faith, I can." The third statement goes on to say: "Your faith is no better than a demon's faith because even the demons believe in one God—and they shudder!" They have some reaction; they don't have faith, but they have a reaction.

It is the second and third sayings that are such a puzzle to the commentators, one of whom said: "The interpretations of this difficult verse are very numerous and for the most part highly subtle and unsatisfactory." That was the best commentary I could lay my hands on. He is baffled. He then takes four pages of tiny print to give all the interpretations there have been, and none of them is satisfactory.

So these few verses are a real problem. What is said is clear enough, but who said it is not at all clear. I have wrestled with this. I have written to other preachers and told them my problem, but none of them could help me. I am going to give you my conclusion, which is that all three statements are from the heckler, the objector, and that when he says "you" and "your" he is referring to James, and to James's claim that faith without works is dead. That is the best I can do.

The first statement, we know, is the statement of the objector. In this he separates faith and works and regards them as two different things. He says to James, "You have faith, I have works." Actually that is quite a common objection, especially of unbelievers, but even of some believers. They say, "I'm not a theologian." Have you heard believers say that? Of course they are! Every believer is a theologian because theology is what you think about God and every believer has thoughts about God. But they say, "I'm not a theologian, I'm just a practising Christian, I just *do* it."

I have never meant this seriously, but I have said that my wife and I are good partners – I preach and she practises, and the two go together beautifully. That is not fair at all on either of us. But there are Christians that say this kind of thing and who say, "I may not have faith, but I have works; I do it." So this objector is actually separating faith and works and saying you can have one without the other. He is saying: you are the theologian, you have the faith, you have the doctrine, I just get on and I do it. But that is quite a statement to make. You can see that he has made a very foolish mistake already in suggesting that James is thinking of faith and work as two entirely separate things. He is saying, "You have the one and I have the other, and that's it." That is easy enough to understand.

But then there is the second statement: "You show me your faith without works and I'll show you mine with works." Is that James talking or is it the objector talking? I think it is still the objector. Not least because he has the same direct address "you" (*su* in the Greek) and it is emphatic in each case. I think he is still attacking James. What he is saying is this: you have faith, I have works; you can't demonstrate your faith to anybody else, you can't let them see it; it is all inside. But he said: I can show people what I believe by what I do; I can show people my faith by my works.

Now when he says "my faith" we don't know what he is really saying. We don't know if he shares James's faith or not. What he is really saying is what unbelievers have said to me: "You have this doctrinal faith, but I'm just a do-good Christian and I get on with it, and therefore I show people what I believe by what I do." What he believes may or may not be the full Christian faith. But he is making the point that you cannot demonstrate a faith without works, which is exactly what James was trying to say. So it ceases to be a real objection.

But he is saying that to demonstrate your faith you have got to have works. He is almost implying: but you don't really need faith. You show by what you do what you really believe, and that is the important thing. So though it could be James's reply, I don't think he would say "Show me your faith" to a man who has just said, "I don't have faith, I have works." Therefore I think it is still the objector saying: you can't demonstrate a faith without works, but I will show you what I believe by my works.

Let us move to the third statement. Here there is a very definite ridiculing of faith without works. It is saying: "What do you believe?" Now a Jew has a creed taken from Deuteronomy 6:3 – "Hear O Israel, the Lord our God, the Lord is one." It immediately goes on to say, "And you shall love the Lord your God with all your heart, with all your strength...." and we often quote that second part. But he is saying: if you believe in one God, so do all the demons in hell. They do have a reaction to it, they do shudder. The literal word is they "bristle". Their hairs stand on end. Now we know this from the Gospels, that the demons again and again said to Jesus: "We're afraid of you." They trembled before Jesus. The demons believe in one God, which is everything the Jews believe in. The Jews have made that verse in Deuteronomy their creed, calling it the "Shammah".

Only three religions of the world do that: Christianity, Judaism, and Islam. That is why there is a move afoot to bring those three religions together. Muslims want that, some Jews want it, and some Christians are even falling for it. But the fact that we all believe in one God is not the important issue. The far more important thing is what kind of one God do you believe in. Simple monotheism is not really important; it is not life-changing just to believe in one God. It can be the opposite. It can lead to fear of God if you believe in one God and nothing else. The demons believe in one God and they bristle. Their hair stands on end and they are afraid of that one God. In other words, this is saying: "What use is your faith?"

Again, I think it must be an objector saying this because why would James respond to a man who says, "I don't have faith but I have works," with the statement "Your faith is no better than the demons"? I don't follow. But if it is the objector talking to James still, I can understand. He is saying: your faith in one God doesn't make any difference. That is true. So I must leave you with this conundrum. I believe that up to this point, the end of v. 19, it is still the objector making three criticisms of the man he thinks only has faith. Funnily enough, he is half agreeing with James. James has specifically said faith without works is no use. What the objector is saying is, "Faith isn't any use anyway, what you need are works."

Now have I left you in utter confusion? Maybe you never noticed this before and where the punctuation marks came. I can only leave you with what I think is happening, but please do not take that as "gospel truth", as they say. Don't think

I am infallible, I am not the pope. I have no ambition to be and no ambition to be taken as the last word on scripture. I have said it before and I say it again to you now: don't believe anything I say if you can't find it for yourself in the scripture. That is my safety. I am just one of God's teachers of his Word, and no teacher is infallible. The commentaries are not infallible. I have got plenty of them! The only infallible book I have got is the Bible. When it is uncertain I am uncertain, and that is all there is to say.

So having claimed that this was the argument from the objector I move on to the answer to his argument. As soon as I move on to v. 20 I get confirmation that what I have been saying is perhaps the best interpretation because at this point James is saying "You empty man!" He uses the word "empty", hollow minded, silly. The literal word is "vain", but not vain in the sense of proud, vain in the sense of empty, hollow. When James writes that, he is saying: all your arguments are based on the wrong supposition, so let us go right back to what I am really saying – you foolish man, do you really want to know what I am saying? Do you really want to be convinced? It is a challenge to a man who is making objections for the sake of making objections. That is why I believe that the punctuation marks in the NIV are wrong and that they should have gone right on to the end of v. 19. Then James comes back and says: O foolish man! Empty-headed man, do you really want to be convinced of what I'm saying? Do you really want the truth or are you just arguing for the sake of arguing?

That is how I understand it. That gives me a clue that all those statements so far are empty-headed statements that are said without really thinking, and they are objecting to James's basic claim.

James wants to give the proof that what he is saying is real. You have got the wrong end of the stick; you have misunderstood the point. You really are arguing from entirely different premises.

To answer this man with proof he goes to his Bible. His Bible, being in the early days of the church, was the Jewish Bible. Never forget that the early church had the verbal New Testament but not the written.

So James goes back to the written Old Testament for his proof. That is James's essential stand. He is a Jew, he believes in the Old Testament as the Word of God, as we should do. He goes back to two people in the Old Testament: Abraham and Rahab. What a contrast! Two more different people he could hardly have picked. One is a man, one is a woman. One is a man in the chosen people of God, future Jews, and the other is a woman who is a Canaanite, a Gentile. Abraham is a respectable man, a farmer; he is looked up to. Rahab is a woman of the streets, looked down on by everybody. He could not have chosen a greater contrast.

Do you know the stories of these two? You know about Abraham, but you might not be as familiar with Rahab, who is recorded at the beginning of the book of Joshua. So it is not part of the Jewish Torah (the first five books of the Bible, revered by the Jews more than any other books in the Old Testament and referred to as the Law of Moses.

So one of these people is taken out of the law, the Torah, and the other is taken from scriptures outside the Torah. It is almost as if James is saying: I want you to realise the breadth of salvation and the different people that you will find inside God's people – because Rahab became part of the chosen people. Both Abraham and Rahab became ancestors of King David, and the son of David, our Lord Jesus Christ. If you read Matthew 1, there is Abraham and there is Rahab. It is remarkable how these two totally different people found their way into God's people, and into the family tree of the Lord Jesus Christ.

So that is the contrast and therefore the comparison is more important still. What did they have in common? What did they share that led them to the position they later held? The answer is that they both had a faith that worked. They both put their faith to work. They both did something that made their faith real. When Abraham sacrificed Isaac, God had told him to do that. God had promised that, "Through Isaac you will have more descendants than you can imagine, more than the sand on the seashore, more than the stars in the sky." Yet, later, God said, "Now I want you to sacrifice your only beloved son, and to do it on Mount Moriah"– which later became known as Calvary or Golgotha, and it is very interesting how it ties up with the death of Jesus. But the main point is that God was asking Abraham to kill off his only hope for the future. What a test of his faith to believe God in those circumstances, when his only hope of having a nation of descendants was this one son, and God says, "Kill him." He went on his way to do just that – what a test of his faith. Even on the way, the son who was carrying a bundle of wood for the fire said, "We've got the wood for the fire, but we've got no lamb, no sheep to sacrifice." We are simply told the Lord will provide. Then there must have been a moment of horror when Abraham, the father, lifted up the knife to kill his son on the altar. It was at that point that an angel told Abraham, "Stop! It's alright! It was a test of your faith and that's all it was meant to be, so you don't need to kill the boy." Then comes one of the most interesting remarks in the Bible. When I have drawn attention to it I have been hounded. But it says then that God says to Abraham: "Now I know that you fear me." "Now I know" – but doesn't God know everything before? No. He didn't know – but, "now" he does. There is a little insight into a very profound, huge question, which we cannot go into now. The question is: does God know everything we are going to do? He knows everything we can do and its outcome. But he says to Abraham: "Now I know...." Not only did he know, but Abraham knew as well. When he acted on his faith he had made his faith sure. God was now sure of Abraham and Abraham was sure of God in stopping the sacrifice. Both were sure of each other, which they had not been before.

I will leave that huge question for a philosophical seminar. But let us get back to the issue. That was Abraham. He risked his entire future in obedience to God. His faith was tested to the extreme and he passed the test. Here James is saying: do you see how his deeds, his works, his actions co-operated with his faith and completed his faith? Now notice those two verbs. Faith and works "co-operated" and the works "completed" his faith, and those are very important words. The word "co-operated" is a translation of a Greek word, "synergy", or "together work". It is a word about doing something together. Paul says that we are co-workers with God; for Abraham his works and his faith worked together and God was sure of his faith from that moment. His faith was completed by his works and his faith was a co-operation between faith and works. That is what James is saying right now. He is saying: Is your faith complete? Are your works co-operating with your faith? Do your actions take risks for God? And then you will know, and God will know, that you really do believe in him. We will return to that point in the next chapter.

Let's go on to Rahab. Again, she put her faith into action. She did something about it. Joshua 2 records the incident. The people of Israel have crossed the Jordan and are now camping just inside the Promised Land. Interestingly enough, God parted the Jordan for this generation as he parted the Red Sea for the previous generation. He had to repeat it for them because most of them were not alive when they went through the Red Sea. In fact, all but two of the earlier generation were dead. So he repeats the separation of the waters and they walk on dry land through to the Promised Land. Incidentally, he has to take them through the Ten Commandments all over again too. So the Ten Commandments are in Deuteronomy as well as Exodus. The word "Deuteronomy" means second law: ("deutero" = second; "nomos" = law), so the "Second Law" is given to them, the same Ten Commandments plus a lot of others, as they were the first time. Do you see what God was doing? An entire generation has died in the wilderness as punishment for their lack of faith. So God has a new generation and he separates the water for them, brings them through dry land, to the Promised Land, but only just, and facing them is a heavily fortified city, Jericho. That is their first objective to take. If they don't take Jericho they won't get any further. It guarded the very place where they were to cross the Jordan.

You know the account of the walls of Jericho falling down at the sound of trumpets and the shouting of "Halleluiah!" But one part of the wall did not fall down. It was the section on which a house was actually built on the wall. It was a brothel run by a prostitute named Rahab. It was right on the side facing the camp of the Israelites. Joshua sent in two spies and said, "Go and find out what's happening in the city and come back and tell us how it is going to be taken, or how difficult it will be."

So the two spies came into the city and (I think quite acutely) decided to seek a bed in the brothel as the least likely place to be discovered. Rahab took them in. It was heard that there were spies who had got in and the police came to search. Rahab took the spies up to the roof and hid them under a pile of flax which was drying in the sun. The police challenged Rahab: "Have the spies come in here? Neighbours say they saw two men who were not men of Jericho." She said, "No, they've already left," a straight lie by the way, as she had hidden them under the flax.

She not only gave the Israelite spies a bed for the night, but she said, "I suggest when you leave the town that you go east towards the mountains. Don't rush straight back to the Israelites. Go east and I'll tell them you went back to the camp, west" – a second lie. What I am saying is that neither Abraham nor Rahab were perfect people. They are both recorded as telling lies to save their own skin. So she sent them west up into the mountains instead of east back to camp yet told them she had seen them go east. So they charged out to go and follow them back to camp and capture them before they got back. But they found no one, of course.

Then she said: "Then after three days slip around Jericho and you'll get back to the camp." So she saved their lives. The reason she did so is there in Joshua 2. She said, "We've all heard about what your God has done for you," and she mentions the separation in the Red Sea. She said, "We're all afraid of you because we think your God is going to give you this city" – which he was. But she added to that her faith and she said, "It's your God I believe in." Then she said, "When you take this city" – not *if* you take it, but *when* you take it – "will you please be kind to my family?" She had let them out of the window on the wall on a rope when they fled up into the mountains. They said, "Hang a scarlet cord from your window and we'll see it and if your family is gathered in that room they'll be safe." So it turned out the walls all fell down except one bit, and it was her house. It stayed up with a scarlet cord hanging from the window. It is a wonderful account.

Now what had that in common with Abraham? Very simply, she risked her whole future. She risked her life and she did it because she believed in the God of Israel. It is thrilling. Abraham and Rahab were not concerned with giving food and drink to the hungry and the naked, that is a work of love. What they were concerned with was their faith, their trust and their obedience. They both acted on their faith and therefore both were justified and both became friends of God.

Though, actually, the title "Friend of God" was given to Abraham not immediately but years later, by two prophets who called him that. Still to this day all the Muslims call Abraham the friend of God. What a title to have! How did he get it? He got it by believing and acting on his faith. So the conclusion comes again – for the fifth time in just thirteen verses James makes this clear assertion and claim. He has answered the arguments; he has given his own arguments, so now he comes back to the basic thought: faith without works is as dead as a corpse, it cannot save, it can't do you any good at all, and it certainly wouldn't do anybody else any good at all.

That is the conclusion that is the most argued statement from James's letter. In the next chapter I deal with the theology. Isn't that statement a contradiction of Paul's teaching? Can we accept both Paul and James on faith and works? Paul says specifically: "We are saved by faith. That is the gift of God, not of works lest any man should boast."

I am quoting just one of Paul's statements to that effect. We will look at the other statements. Is there not here a straight contradiction? Doesn't Paul teach we are justified by faith alone and does not James say the exact opposite? You can see he says that a man is justified by his works and not by faith alone. This is where most evangelicals hit the buffers and rise up in horror. Some of them say, as Martin Luther did, that you can't contradict Paul.

6
FAITH AND WORKS (2)

Read James 2:14 –26

A. PROBLEM
  1. Paul (v. James)
  2. Augustine (v. Pelagius)
  3. Luther + Calvin (v. Arminius)
B. SOLUTION
  1. Contradictory – opposite
  (evangelicals choose faith, liberals works)
  2. Compatibility – same
  (faith should produce good works of love)
  3. Complementary – different
  (active faith)

FAITH WITHOUT ACTIONS	v. FAITH WITH ACTIONS
Believing THAT	Believing IN
Professed	Practised
Words (creed)	Works (conduct)
Passive (mind) Think	Active (will) do
Truth	Trust
Incomplete (can't save)	Complete (do save)

C. QUESTIONS
  1. Does saying "sinners" prayer save?
  2. When did you FIRST believe?
  3. When did you LAST believe?

Now we tackle this passage from a very different angle – theologically. There is a big problem with chapter 2. I remember vividly the American astronauts on their way to the moon who said, "Houston, we have a problem." What an understatement! Part of the space vehicle had exploded and was lost, but fortunately they got back safely. Theologians who read this second half of James 2 say we have a problem, and it's a big one. Very simply stated, it is nothing less than an apparent contradiction in the New Testament, where Paul seems to say one thing and James says the opposite.

It is a real problem for those who believe in the inspiration and authority of scripture, especially for those who follow Paul as their main heavyweight in theology. Most evangelicals have probably made Paul their major source of truth and judge the rest of the New Testament in light of his letters. Others do it the other way around. James was the Lord's stepbrother, presiding elder over the Jerusalem church, which was the mother church in the early days. Paul, as you know, was the missionary to the Gentiles and wrote more of the New Testament than anybody else.

But they are both in the New Testament and they knew each other. They had both taken part in the famous Jerusalem Council in Acts 15 where Paul, in his mission to Gentiles, was arguing that they did not need to become Jews to believe in the Jewish Messiah, and therefore did not need to be circumcised. James, as the Jewish leader of the Jewish church in Jerusalem, chaired the debate, and if you read Acts 15 you know the outcome. This is not a secondary matter, this is about salvation. The most fundamental subject in the New Testament is: what must I do to be saved? Paul apparently says: nothing except believe. James says: you'd better add works to your belief or it won't save you. Which is right?

James has made five statements in this one section of chapter 2, in just thirteen verses. Five times he states categorically that faith without works cannot save; faith without works is dead; faith without works is no good at all. Yet Paul says: We are saved by grace through faith; and that not of yourselves; it is the gift of God. He says the exact opposite. Followers of Paul have gone along with Paul rather than James. It was for this reason that Martin Luther and others have played down James and just don't get what he is after, because they are so full of what Paul has said that James can't really get a look in.

There are three possible ways of handling this problem. But I think before we do it might be wise to read just three portions of Paul to hear what Paul has to say about this. The first is in Romans chapter 4:1–2. Notice that both Paul and James appeal to Abraham as the ground of what they are teaching. So Paul writes: "What then shall we say that Abraham, our father, discovered in this matter? If in fact Abraham was justified by works, he had something to boast about, but not before God. What does the Scripture say? 'Abraham believed God, and it was credited to him as righteousness.'"

Notice the words "credited to him". That is what "justified" means. That is justification he is talking about. He says "not of works". Later in chapter 4 he points out that that statement about Abraham's faith (and it was credited to him for righteousness) was said before Abraham did anything, before he circumcised himself and the others – before he did anything about it God credited him with righteousness. That is what Paul says. Interestingly enough, James appeals to the same statement (which is in Genesis 15:6) to prove his point – that faith plus works is needed for justification.

Now look at Galatians 3:6–8. "Consider Abraham, 'He believed God and it was credited to him as righteousness.'" There is the same verse from Genesis. "Understand then that those who believe are children of Abraham. The scripture foresaw that God would justify the Gentiles by faith and announced the gospel in advance to Abraham, 'All nations will be blessed through you.' So those who have faith are blessed along with Abraham, the man of faith."

Then we turn to Ephesians 2 and we read the verses I have quoted already. "For it is by grace you have been saved through faith. And this not from yourselves; it is the gift of God, not by works, so that no one can boast." The next verse is: "We are God's workmanship, created in Christ Jesus to do good works, which God prepared in advance for us to do." Now those three quotes from Paul tell you his position. It is that it is by faith on its own that we are justified, whereas James says the exact opposite. Both of them appeal to Abraham. Both of them quote the same verse from Genesis – that Abraham believed God and it was reckoned, credited to him as righteousness.

However, they interpret that verse differently. Paul interprets that verse to mean that right then, immediately, God accepted Abraham on his faith and from that moment he was justified. James does not interpret it that way. He interprets that statement as a prophecy which was fulfilled later. So there is a difference of interpretation. Paul says it happened right then, Abraham was justified. He makes a point: that was said to him before he did anything with his faith. But James is saying he was justified when his faith was completed, when he did something about it and sacrificed his son. So there is a real difference. Can't both be right? Well let us see if we can find a way of bringing them together. Superficially, you have to say they can't both be right; there is a direct contradiction. But we are going to go deeper and we are raising a huge question which is relevant to us. What must I do to be saved? What must you do to be saved? James says faith plus works, Paul says faith only.

What do you do? This affects all our evangelism and how

we lead others to Christ. Now forgive me for going through the church's history down the centuries just a little, because this issue has been a controversy in the church ever since. It boils down to this question: who does the saving? Does God do it all or do we have something to contribute? When a person is saved today, is that all God's doing or has that person co-operated with God and contributed something to his salvation? That is a huge issue. The first time it surfaced in church history was in the fifth century with Augustine, a bishop in North Africa. You may have heard his testimony in his *Confessions*. He took the line that salvation is all God's doing, it is not our doing at all. Of course this led to an extraordinary series of implications. It meant that God chooses who is to be saved. We don't make any choice, it is he who chooses us, and he chooses some to be saved and some not to be. He chooses some for heaven and others he leaves for hell. Now that is an extraordinary position, but Augustine was the first really to take it. It is because he believed in the use of force. He built an awful lot on a text in the parable of the great feast, where the owner of the feast says, "Go into the byways and highways and force people to come in" (*persuade* is one translation; *compel* is another).

Therefore he saw God's grace as an irresistible force which compelled people to be saved whether they chose to be or not. He began to teach that repentance and faith are not something we do at all, but something that God does in us. Therefore it is not up to me to do anything; God will produce repentance in me, he will produce faith in me. He even went so far as to say that you must be born again before you repent and believe, because otherwise you could not do either. Now these are quite radical things to say.

As the first man to take that line, Augustine was highly critical of a British monk called Pelagius, who went to Rome to live. He was horrified by the decadence of the

Roman churches – no holiness. So he swung to the opposite extreme and said: it is up to you, and the lack of effort means the lack of holiness – you need to do this. Therefore he put much emphasis on human responsibility, in reaction to Augustine's emphasis on divine responsibility. I would agree that Pelagius was wrong. He said we didn't all get born with sin in us; we were all born innocent and we chose sin, we are entirely responsible for what we are.

Now this is the basic issue: who is responsible for saving people? Augustine said God is – entirely. Pelagius took the opposite view and said it is a person's own fault if they are going to hell. It is someone's own responsibility to accept Christ as their Saviour. Therefore he put all of it on the human will. I am simplifying this to try to make it clear to you. However, there was a bunch of French bishops in between the two. They said: salvation is a combination of what God does and what we do; he saves, we do the repenting and believing, and the result is salvation. God calls us and we call on him for salvation. It is both; it is a matter of co-operation.

To put it as simply as I can to get this across, it is the difference between: (a) believing that we have drowned and therefore we can do nothing for ourselves and God rescues us; *or* (b) that we are drowning and somebody is throwing a lifebelt to us and telling us to grab hold of it and he will then pull us to the shore; *or* (c) that we are strong swimmers and are not drowning at all and just need to decide to swim to the shore. Does that make that clear to you? The French bishops said the gospel is God is throwing us a lifeline and it is our responsibility to grab it and hold on until he pulls us to the shore.

Unfortunately, Augustine was a very clever man and he labelled the French bishops semi-Pelagian. You could have just as easily called them semi-Augustinian! That finished them off in many people's eyes because the church accepted

Augustine, and he is regarded as the greatest Church Father of all, though I am afraid I can never think that. I come firmly in the middle with the French bishops. You can call me semi-Pelagian or semi-Augustinian – both apply. I believe it is both God's responsibility and our responsibility, and that we need to preach the gospel emphasising both. Nobody can save themselves, nobody can earn salvation, nobody can deserve it – that is grace. But grace needs to be accepted and used, and it is our responsibility to do just that. To try to make that even clearer, you could think of asking people who hold any of the three views whose fault is it that some people are not being saved. For it is very obvious that not all are being saved. The Augustinian would say it is entirely God's choice; it is his responsibility that many are not being saved. Pelagius would say it is entirely man's choice and our responsibility. People in the middle would say: it is both; we need to hear God's call and we need to call on him. In Acts 2, for example, as you find all through the New Testament, there is this combination of God's responsibility and ours. It does not mean that we can save ourselves but it does mean that it is our responsibility if we are not saved.

Now that was how the tension between James and Paul surfaced in the fifth century. Let us turn the pages of history quite quickly to the Reformation. I have to say that Luther was an Augustinian monk and Calvin was a student of Augustine, and his magnificent two tomes called *The Institutes of the Christian Religion* are little more than a systematic Augustinian view. So the major Protestant Reformers were on the Augustinian side of this question.

You find that there was another point of view, the Anabaptists' particularly. They and others said: human responsibility is real; it is not all God's responsibility that people are not being saved, it is partly ours. Therefore they taught that being saved is the result of God's decision and ours, that the two are needed and that there is a co-operation between the two.

This resulted in a Reformed theology which has high-lighted this because it has over-emphasised the responsibility of God for salvation and under-emphasised the human part in being saved. Therefore it tends to emphasise faith in God's part, and not works, which are man's part. That is where the tensions of faith and works really reached a head. The result was that Reformed theology added a word to Paul which he never used. It was the word "alone" – "sola" in Latin, *sola fides*, faith alone. That word is never in any of Paul's letters, but it is assumed that it is what he taught. It was added by the Reformers, later the Puritans, and is used today by many Reformed preachers. But remember that Paul never actually used it. The only person who ever used the term "faith alone" was James. He said: it is *not* by faith alone. But he was not directly contradicting Paul because Paul never said it was by faith alone. That is the first key point for us to note.

Let us bring this right up to date. Those who believe that salvation is God's responsibility and not ours tend also today to believe and preach "once saved, always saved." That is because their argument is that if God has done all the work of salvation he will keep you. It is all his responsibility; perseverance is his work in you, not your work. That is why Calvinism as such believes in the perseverance of the saints. What they mean by that is it is God's responsibility to keep you as well as to save you – it is all of God. That is why I wrote a little book entitled *Once Saved, Always Saved?* (note the question mark in the title) which is proving extremely popular—if that is the right word—and it is going into other languages. It was published by Hodder and Stoughton who also published a book entitled *Once Saved, Always Saved* without a question mark by no less a man than R.T. Kendall who was minister of Westminster Chapel. I tell people buy and read both books, and then go back to the Bible.

I point out in my book that there are over eighty passages in your New Testament that tell you that you can lose your salvation and that you have a duty to keep up your side of the relationship, and I firmly believe that. But the majority of Reformed teachers and preachers today would disagree profoundly with me. I am trying to make this a real issue for you so that you realise it has profound implications for how you get saved today. On the day of Pentecost the disciples were confronted with a question: "What must we do?" According to the Augustinian-Calvinist side they should have been told, "Nothing." They should have been told, "Only believe." But they were not, they were told to repent, they were told to get baptised for the forgiveness of sins. They were given an honest, straight answer to the straight question "what must we do?" – "You need to do this." They did it, and three thousand were saved that day because they did what they were told to do.

I have told you that "do" is the main key word in the Epistle of James. You can see why it is not terribly popular among Reformed theologians. They don't really like to preach from it. James is saying God will do his bit if you do yours. There are things that he can do and will do for you if you do your bit. If you repent and believe, he will save. It is as simple as that. But it is a huge issue with so many Christians today, and I have tried to show you how it is. Nothing we can do can merit salvation, let us be clear about that. You can do nothing that makes you deserve to be saved. You can do nothing to get something in God's credit account for you. Faith is the only thing that will get you into credit with God – that is the meaning of Genesis 15:6. I am trying to put this so simply and clearly that you really understand.

In the eighteenth century the whole thing came up again between two of the greatest evangelists of that period, John

Wesley and George Whitfield. The latter left his evangelism in charge of John Wesley and said, "I'm heading off for America." He was instrumental in the beginning of the great revival in the middle of the next century in America. But Whitfield and Wesley profoundly disagreed over this whole question of who does the saving. Wesley was very clear that it is a question of both. We have something to do and God has something to do, and it is only when those two get together that salvation is the result.

So they had this great difference in the nineteenth century and it has lasted until today. If I were to put Billy Graham on one side and Martin Lloyd Jones on the other, I would not be far off. The real question is what must we do, and I believe the clear answer of Scripture; there are things that you must do if you want to be saved. They will not merit salvation, they will not deserve it, they will not earn it. It is all of grace. But grace does not force itself on anybody. Grace is for those who are willing to receive it and live by it. When I speak in Singapore that is now my main burden, because there is a teaching coming out of there in our day which is being spread through the mass media and widely accepted because it is a popular message: that is that you don't need to do anything, grace is free.

But then the question remains, why then is grace not reaching everybody? It is not God's fault because the gospel of grace is being freely distributed around the whole world by mass media, yet still people refuse. The truth is grace is not an irresistible force. Grace is an undeserved favour which you can refuse and which you can turn down, and you grieve the Holy Spirit when you do. But you are free to refuse the gospel; you are free to turn it down. That is, I am afraid, the truth – and why many are not saved today, especially in rich countries.

There are three possible solutions and they centre

around three words: contradictory, compatibility, and complementary (meaning that they support one another). Now the first solution to the tension between James and Paul is to accept that they are contradictory, as many Christians have done. That forces a choice on you as to which you prefer, and which you believe, and which you will live by, and which will save you. When you have a choice between James and Paul, some people prefer James and many others prefer Paul. Who prefers James? Well the liberals on the whole prefer James because it panders to human pride. That is because if you can decide your salvation, if it is up to you, you can say, "I decided to become a Christian; I chose it all, it was all me; it was my choice, my decision." That really keeps your pride. You don't have to come and say, "Nothing in my hand I bring, simply to the cross I cling." That is very humbling to sing or to say. It is what we call the "do-gooding" kind of Christianity. The number of people who have said to me, "I'm as good as anyone who goes to your church." You have heard it, haven't you? The more good you do the more proud you are. There are a lot of people even in church who are relying on the good things they have done.

I was once asked to go and speak to the Baptist Women's League. I confess that is not my scene. I went, and I met this rather overpowering lady who said, "I'm taking the chair. What are you going to speak on?"

I replied, "I'm going to speak on grace."

"Oh, that sounds nice," she said.

"Well, I'm going to say two things. Grace means first of all that your bad deeds need not keep you out of heaven." She brightened up and smiled at that. I continued: "The second point I want to make is that your good deeds won't help you to get there."

That I am afraid was the wrong thing to say to her. She got quite flighty and said, "Are you trying to tell me that all my good deeds are wasted?"

I replied, "They weren't wasted as far as other people are concerned, they helped other people, but they won't help you a bit."

She never spoke to me again, and I was never invited back to the Baptist Women's League. However, grace means your bad deeds need not keep you out of heaven, but your good deeds won't help you to get there. Liberals prefer a gospel that says you can save yourself.

Funnily enough, Peter on the day of Pentecost said, "Save yourselves from this wicked generation". Save yourselves! He was then pointing to the responsibility there is on humans to do their part, and, when they wanted to know what it was, he said, "Repent and be baptised." That doesn't make you feel proud. Repenting kills your pride because you are admitting that you are a sinner, you are admitting that you have done wrong. But when you come to Christ you even need to repent of your good deeds. Did you ever realise that? You need to leave all the good things you have done behind because they are not going to help.

Do you understand that? You need to repent of all your deeds, good and bad, and leave them behind and come as a sinner who needs to repent and who needs to believe and who needs to be baptised. When you put all the responsibility on God for your salvation you tend to downplay repentance, because repentance is surely something you do. You tend to downplay faith and you misquote what Paul said about it.

When Paul wrote, "By grace are we saved through faith ... and that not of yourselves," what does "not of yourselves" refer to? It does not refer to the faith. That is the biggest mistake people make. Grammatically its case belongs to the word "saved" in the previous argument. So what Paul is saying in, "It's not of yourselves" is not faith but the salvation part: "For by grace you are saved. And that not of yourselves, through faith." Now anybody with Greek can check me up on that. But the words "not of yourselves" grammatically connect with *saved*, not with *faith*.

But so many have taken that verse to mean that faith is something God does. No, you need to *believe*. Again and again in the New Testament people are told, "Believe on the Lord Jesus and you will be saved." It is an imperative, a command. You do the believing and he will do the saving. It is so important. This faith is not a gift of God. Faith is something we do. That is James's point too. But do you see how easy it is to mistake a scripture and get it wrong?

So evangelicals prefer Paul. Why? Because the only thing you need to do to get saved is believe, and that is so simple – just believe and you are saved. So many evangelistic crusades are based on just that. But James will have none of that. So true evangelicals are still left with a problem which is that both Paul and James are in the New Testament and they are both inspired by God and they both have something to say.

So the first thing people have done with this apparent contradiction is to have accepted that it is *contradictory*. I don't accept that. Evangelicals choose Paul and liberals choose James. But we don't choose between them, we accept both as the inspired Word of God. So that is not the solution. The second solution that people have come to is *compatibility*. They try to make out that Paul and James are both saying the same thing. They usually begin with Paul and point out that Paul is very keen on good works too – that Paul believed justifying faith should lead to sanctifying faith; that being credited with righteousness should lead to becoming righteous, the one imputed and later imparted to you, to give the technical terms.

In other words, Paul in Ephesians 2 says we are not saved by good works, but we are saved for good works and good works should follow faith. Therefore many evangelical commentaries I have read say that James and Paul are saying exactly the same thing – that faith should lead to good works or it is not real faith. At first sight that sounds as if the problem is solved. Most evangelical commentaries I have read take this line and feel there is no contradiction at all, that they are actually saying the same thing, that good works do matter, but that they follow faith and they should come from faith and should be a product of faith. In other words, they come *later* than faith. Faith comes first and works follow, works that the Lord has prepared for us beforehand, works that he wanted us to do. Well now that sounds as if we have found the answer. But such is not the case.

I cannot help mentioning one answer which has come to the surface in a book by R.T. Kendall entitled *Justification by Works*. He takes a completely different line to everybody else and says that justification is justification before people, not before God, and if you want to justify your faith to other people it had better be accompanied by good works. That was a unique and totally original way around the problem. Since he followed Martin Lloyd Jones during his lifetime he went to Martin Lloyd Jones with his solution. Apparently, so he says, Martin Lloyd Jones accepted this new insight as the answer to the problem. But it was only one man's solution and one man's agreement and I do not believe it is the right one.

I come to the third solution. Paul and James are not saying the same thing, nor are they contradicting each other. The solution I want to present to you is that they are saying different things that don't contradict each other but are *complementary*, supplementing each other. They are both contributing to the New Testament doctrine of faith, but in different ways. James is adding a dimension to saving faith which Paul did not include in all that he said about faith.

So we need both of them together to understand what faith really is. There is a real difference and they are not saying the same thing. Each is saying something about faith that the other has not said. With every doctrine, if you want the whole New Testament doctrine of a thing you need the whole New Testament. You need to put together all that the New Testament says on a subject to understand it. I could take so many examples of this. I have written a book on divorce. If you are going to understand the New Testament attitude toward divorce and remarriage you need to look at everything that has been said on it. If you look at just one Gospel, Luke, or Mark, you will come to one conclusion. But you need to look at Matthew. Matthew is the only one that includes exceptions to that, which you need to take into account. You need to study what Paul wrote in 1 Corinthians 7. Only when you pull together everything in the New Testament on a subject can you have a reliable understanding of the matter. That is why we have four Gospels. We need them all. If you want to understand Jesus properly you need to study all four. Each has a unique thing to say about Jesus. John has more unique things to say than the other three. You need everything about Jesus. You also need the book of Revelation to understand Jesus as he really is. Many neglect the book of Revelation and get a one-sided view of Jesus, that he is all kindness and meekness, and never gets angry. Revelation gives you a very different view of Jesus, and you need it all. Having pointed that out, if you are to understand faith you need both what Paul said and what James said, and then you will understand true faith, saving faith, justifying faith.

What was wrong with that second answer was that all those answers are fitting James into Paul and making him say the same thing, and they are not saying the same thing. There are other things wrong with that middle answer too. Those who give the middle answer are confusing sanctification with justification. Or, to put it quite simply, they are thinking that "works" always means good deeds. James is careful never to describe works as "good works". Those are works of love, works of kindness. But James is talking about *works of faith*, and that is not works of kindness. Neither Abraham's nor Rahab's were works of kindness, they were works of faith. So let us come to this complementary answer. James is contrasting two kinds of faith – faith that doesn't work and faith that does work. That is what he means by faith with works or faith without works. Faith that is not active, but passive is what he means by faith without works. He is saying both are needed. We need both to be saved. Saving faith is faith that works.

Now this is the definition of faith that I want to spell out. This is a faith with content. Faith without actions has content but it lacks confidence. Faith that works has confidence. I think I will have to start in a very simple way. I was preaching in a church in Hanover, Germany. I asked the congregation, "How many of you believe in me?" Only about half a dozen hands went up. I said, "Well, how many believe that I exist?" And every hand went up. You have got to word the appeal rightly to get a response! There was a well-dressed lady sitting in the front row. She looked as if she was game for a bit of fun so I said to her, "Now you put your hand up to say you believe in me. I don't know if you do. You've professed that you believe in me but you've not done anything about it. If you give me your money to look after, I'll know that you believe in me."

A deathly hush came over the whole congregation as people froze. I thought, "I've said the wrong thing. I don't know what I've said." I asked the pastor afterwards, "Why did they all freeze when I said that?" He said, "She is the richest woman in Hanover. Her husband owns most of the property in the middle of the city and he's died and she's inherited it all." Since we were in a brand new church building I thought: she probably paid for this too. I was trying to teach the people the difference between believing "that" and believing "in". There is a huge difference. She believed "that". She didn't believe "in" me. She certainly looked as if she would never trust me with her money, but that is understandable since she had so much. But are you beginning to see the difference? You do need to have content to your faith. You do need to believe "that" Jesus lived, and died, and rose again, but all that is believing "that". It is a passive belief because it is entirely an internal belief, not something you are doing about it.

But if you are going to have real faith, according to James it must be faith that has *confidence* as well as *content*. This is a very challenging idea, but I think very understandable. There are plenty of people in church who believe "that" the right things. They recite the creed; they believe "that" Jesus was born of a virgin, conceived by the Holy Spirit. They believe "that" he suffered under Pontius Pilate, was crucified, dead and buried. They believe that he rose again and they believe that he ascended to heaven and is going to come back. They say that they believe that, and they do believe that, but it is only half of faith. It is not saving faith; you are believing "that" this happened to Jesus. But believing in him is to run a risk, to risk your future in some way, to behave in such a way that if he is not real you land flat on your face. Do you understand what I am saying? *Real faith is not passive, it is active*. It does something about it. Real faith shows Jesus you trust him. That is why God said to Abraham after he sacrificed Isaac: "Now I know." It is sure now. God was confident after that, as well as Abraham. They were sure of each other. Abraham's faith was completed by what he did about it. James says that then became justifying faith. That was the beginning of salvation, as justifying faith is the beginning of ours. Faith without works is a thing of words. Faith with works is a thing of deeds. Do you see the difference?

Now Paul never said this. If you get all your gospel from Paul you won't include this. But if you believe James has given us the Word of God as well then you need to include this thought in saving faith. You can be a believer of the first sort, without works, for years. Let me ask you some delicate questions. Number one: when did you *first* believe in Jesus? You can probably point to the time when you professed faith. But I am asking you: "When did you first practise faith?" There is a big difference. Think back. Try to think – when did you first believe "in" Jesus and did something that ran a risk for him?

Or let me ask you another question. When did you *last* believe in Jesus? Don't say, "I've always done." That is faith without works – profession. The real question is not whether you *profess* faith in Christ but whether you *possess* faith in Christ; do you *practise* faith in Christ? That is the real test as to whether faith is saving. It does mean, I am afraid, that there are a lot of people in church who have faith but no works, who have never done anything about it. Or put it this way: if you have not done anything about your faith then it can do nothing for you. That is what James is saying. So when did you last believe in Jesus? Can you think of moments in your life when you pinned your faith to him and did something that would have been an awful risk?

My mind immediately goes back to a time when my wife and I were sitting in a train on the border of Romania and I had a huge case full of Christian books and Bibles, which I knew was forbidden. This was when the Iron Curtain was right up. The case was too big to get into the compartment because that was crammed with people, so it was standing in the corridor outside. A horrid lady in a grey uniform, looking like a concentration camp commandant, got on the train and she went through everything with a toothcomb.

She insisted on taking up the cushions of the seats on the train to see if anybody was hiding underneath or whether we were smuggling anything. She searched us, searched the compartment, then she turned and was looking straight at my case in the corridor. I thought, "I'm in for it now." I turned my eyes and said, "Lord, it's time for a miracle." Believe it or not, at that moment a drunken soldier standing in the corridor grabbed a fire extinguisher and set it off and sprayed it into the whole carriage up the corridor and we were covered in clouds of this smoke and dust.

This lady in the grey uniform said, "Off the train!" We had to climb down off the train and stand on the sleepers at the side. It was about twenty minutes before the air cleared and then she said, "Get back on the train." So we got back on the train and there was my case covered in white powder but with everything intact inside. That was how we got into Romania that time. It is a little thing, but I was risking a lot. I had said, "Lord, time for a little miracle." When did you last do that? When was your faith a living faith and not as James says, a dead faith that could only say "I believe that" to everything. The test is whether we believe "in".

It is not a case of faith being something you think in your mind, it is also something you do with your will. It is not just accepting truth, it is trust as well. That is what James is saying. He is writing about the works of faith – what makes faith a living and a saving faith is what you *do* about it. That is my answer to the tension between Paul and James. I think we should be grateful to the Lord for both because they have both added to our understanding of what faith really is.

7
TEACHERS AND TONGUES

Read James 3:1–12

A. DISCOURAGED TEACHERS (1)
 1. Greater authority
 2. Greater accountability
  a. Heresy on lips
  b. Holiness in lives

B. DANGEROUS TONGUES (2-12)
 able to control tongue, whole body
  1. Significance (2) – proof of perfection
  2. Size (3-6)
  – horse's bit, ship's rudder, forest fire
  3. Stubbornness (7-8)
  – wild species, wild speech
   (restless, poisonous)
  4. Schizophrenic (9-12)
   a. Possible in human nature
    – blessing/curse
   b. Impossible in nature
    – spring/tree

A third of the New Testament is made up of letters or epistles, which is the technical name for them. They are correspondence, and if you enjoy reading other people's letters, then the New Testament is an ideal book for you to read. We are listening to one side of a conversation when we read a letter. When people with mobile phones talk loudly in your presence and you can't hear what the other person is saying, does that irritate you as it irritates me? You are only getting one side of a verbal interchange. Let me test it out on you. Here's somebody with a mobile phone: "Hello, is that you? Now, I'm dying to know, has it arrived...? Oh, congratulations! That's wonderful news! How much does it weigh...? What colour is it...? Is it petrol or diesel?" Do you see what I mean? You were only hearing one side of a conversation, and I will bet your minds had jumped to wrong conclusions!

Correspondence corresponds, and when you read a letter in the New Testament your first task is to ask what is going on at the other end. That is how from the epistles you can gauge what is going on in situations to which they wrote. That applies to this: "Not many of you should presume to be teachers." That is a surprising thing to say when you consider that teachers are a gift of the ascended Christ to his church and one of the five major ministries (apostles, prophets, evangelists, pastors, teachers). There are five gifts of the head of the church to his body, though some people say there are only four, regarding pastors and teachers as one gift. I don't think that is so because I have met some pastors who can't teach, and I've met other teachers who can't pastor. It is quite a rare thing to find them both equally in one person, so I regard those as five gifts. Someone can have one, two, or three of those gifts. Why should James appear to be discouraging teachers? Well, the two subjects in James 3 are teachers and tongues, and we will look at both.

You would have thought, since it was one of the major ministries of the church, that the right thing to do would be to encourage people to consider teaching others, but James says the opposite. He does it for the sake of those who would love to be teachers – because, as he says, they will receive stricter judgement than other Christians. We will explain why that is so in a moment. It is obvious that there were too many people putting themselves forward as teachers in the churches which, you recall, were made up of Jewish Christians dispersed among the nations. They had been converted as the dispersed Jews of Israel, and they had gathered in little fellowships, or synagogues. They were used to calling themselves synagogues, and they did so when they were Christians too. As the synagogues had usually had at least one rabbi or teacher, then so did the Christian synagogues made up of converted Jews, and so James is discouraging them. They were getting too full of windbags, people who had a desire to teach the others.

Why should people have such a desire? Quite frankly, there are some rather subtle pleasures in being a teacher, such is human nature. We can enjoy correcting other people or informing them, and knowing things that others do not know, and telling them. It happens in ordinary gossip. People enjoy passing on things that they are sure others have not heard. There is a certain pleasure in being "in the know" and in correcting others. In the flesh, we can enjoy putting others right, and there are subtle temptations of dignity and status because teachers acquire a certain status. There are some people who would like to have that status, and so the first thing that James does is say, "Now don't rush to be teachers. Don't have an ambition to be a teacher."

I remember when I first told our pastor in church, "I feel I ought to be a pastor." He said, "Don't! Stay out of the ministry if you can possibly do so." I thought at first that was rather strange advice, and that he would be keen to chalk up another convert to the ministry, but no! I realise now what wise advice it was. I went back to see him about twelve months later and said, "I have no other choice; I've got to." That is why Paul says, "The love of Christ constrains me. Woe is me if I don't preach." That is the compulsion that comes if it is a clear call from God. It is not a human ambition but a divine calling, and it must be that. It is because not only does that give you greater authority, but it opens you up to greater accountability. "We teachers," and you notice the "we" there – he is saying he is a teacher too, and again he is virtually saying: I didn't have any choice either. I had to be. It does expose. I am exposing myself to stricter judgement than most in the day when God looks at what we have been doing.

Why should that be? There are two obvious reasons. One is that a teacher has the responsibility of interpreting and applying God's word. He doesn't just read it or repeat it, he seeks to interpret it and tell people what it means and then apply it to daily life. Those are the two callings of a teacher. To make the word of God real includes going back into the past, getting its original meaning and its original setting, and then coming back into the present and showing its relevance to daily life now. That is the job of a teacher. All that is summed up in a technical term – *hermeneutics*.

Hermeneutics covers both the interpretation of scripture and its application in today's context. That is the teacher's job, but there are many factors that can creep in to that task of hermeneutics: the preacher's background, the way he was brought up, what he was taught by others. The teacher's temperament plays a big role. Is he an extrovert or an introvert? Does he like challenging people or does he prefer comforting? The people who have taught him will have had a great influence, consciously or unconsciously. The result is that teachers with the same Bible can come up with great variations in both interpretation and application.

There are two very common ways in which teachers can distort the Word of God without realising it. One is by having favourite authors and by letting one writer of the

Bible have more influence on their thinking than the others. Among evangelicals, this particularly applies to Paul. Many evangelicals have taken Paul as their last and final guide to what they believe, and what Paul says goes. We saw in James 2 that he appears to contradict Paul when he says that it is not by faith alone that we are saved, but by faith plus works. That seemed on the face of it the exact opposite of Paul. On any subject, faith included, we must balance all that all the authors say about a subject, and not choose one rather than another. That means studying the whole Bible all the time, and everything it says on any given subject. One of the most common ways in which teachers distort the Word of God is to quote texts out of context. A text without a context becomes a pretext for the teacher's own ideas, prejudices and opinions.

All this can get in the way of the Word of God, and a teacher will be judged by whether he has been faithful to the Word of God in its original meaning and in its application. That is enough to make any teacher tremble before God. I can tell you that if there is one verse in the Bible that makes me tremble, it is James 3:1 – it really does, because you are accountable to God for your teaching to others. It is a heavy responsibility. There is another way in which the teacher will be judged: by his own teaching. You see, God judges everybody by how much they know, and if you don't know a thing, God is prepared to regard that as ignorance. Time and again the Bible says that God overlooks something because of people's ignorance. You remember Jesus' prayer on the cross, "Father, forgive them for they don't know what they're doing." They were ignorant of the gigantic crime of which they could be accused by his Father, and he pleaded that ignorance on their behalf. But a teacher is dedicated to know more than those he teaches.

Mind you, I will let you into a secret. Some people have said to me, "I'm amazed at how much of the whole Bible you know," and the real answer is that I was only one step ahead of the congregation. I knew one chapter better than they did, and gave them that on a Sunday morning. A teacher's real job is to stay one step ahead of those he teaches, so don't get the impression I know it all. Far from it. I am just ahead of you, that is all, and probably not much ahead, but I am qualified to be a teacher because I know a little more than you. That is the main qualification, but knowing more means that I will be judged by more. A teacher will be judged by what he has taught if we arc all judged by what we know. A teacher has dedicated his life to knowing more of the Word of God than other people. That means more judgement, so I am piling up judgement for myself every time I teach. It is quite a sobering thought, and yet I feel I have to teach, that I must do it, that God has said, "You're to be a teacher of my people."

It is great when you know what you are in God's sight. Then you don't try to be what you are not. Hundreds of people have come to faith through my teaching, but I am not an evangelist. I had a year as an evangelist just to prove that I wasn't. It was freedom to know that I am not a Billy Graham, and I am not an evangelist, so I should not try to be. I know I am called to be a teacher, and so I have had to dedicate my time to getting to know God's Word, the whole of it, and what every author says on any subject. Get a balanced view, a biblical view – and it takes a lot of time. I will let you into another secret: preparing to teach any part of the Bible takes me an hour in the study for five minutes' teaching. I have found that if you are not prepared to give that time you are not going to have enough to teach.

So a teacher will be judged by how he has handled the Word and whether he has obeyed it himself – whether he has listened to himself. God has given many of us teachers a gift of wives who hold us to our teaching. It is an uncomfortable thing sometimes when my wife says over the lunch table, "Now you said last Sunday ... and you are not doing it." She is reminding me that God will say one day, "You taught other people to do this and you didn't do it yourself." That is the double reason why teachers will come into stricter judgement than other ministries and giftings in the church. It is a solemn thought for me, not you, unless you share my calling as a teacher of others, whether it is in a house group or a whole church, or whatever. If you are teaching anybody else the Word of God, then you will have a stricter judgement than others in the great day when we all answer to our Maker.

If I said no more on the passage we are considering, that would be enough, a really important lesson for us to learn, but let us move on. The tool that a teacher has to use is the tongue. The rest of this passage is all about this little lump of flesh in our mouths. There was a Church of England vicar who once began his sermon by saying, "I want to show you that part of my body which causes me the greatest temptation," and there was a breathless hush in the congregation. Then he stuck out his tongue to them, and said, "That's what I'm going to talk about. That's the most difficult part of my body to control." Since that is the tool that I have to use, and if you teach others you will have to use it, then we need to know quite a bit about this thing we call the tongue. It is our tool, but it is not only used by a teacher, it is used by every other Christian. Almost every day we are using the tongue, and it is a most dangerous thing to use. I compare it to a mobile saw. You have seen those electric or petrol driven chainsaws that cut down trees which have fallen on the road. That is about the most dangerous machine and you really have to know how to use it. I was once preaching in New Zealand and there was a boy who had been in a very nasty car accident when he was only two years old. It had caused his left arm to be paralysed and therefore it had remained a child-sized arm, and it damaged other parts of his body too. He had very foolishly got hold of a chainsaw to cut up logs, and he was using a chainsaw in one hand and kneeling on a great big log that he was cutting up. He simply sliced his knee right off. Doctors managed to link the bone of his lower leg to the bone in his upper leg without a knee. So here was this poor lad of sixteen sitting in my meeting with a short leg and a short arm, and the Lord had mercy on him and told me that he wanted to heal him. That boy, who was on aluminium crutches, leapt off the crutches and ran outside the shed we were meeting in – he ran right round the field with both arms and legs working, came back into the wool shed, and then gave testimony to the Lord's healing. I have never used a chainsaw, and after meeting that lad I don't think I ever will. They are very dangerous things to handle, and so is your tongue. It is the one part of your body that is the most difficult part to control, so James talks about why it is so dangerous.

The first thing you need to know about your tongue is its significance, which is that it is a gauge, a measurement of how holy you are. It is the quickest way to realise what progress you are making in the Christian life. So much so, that James is prepared to say that if you can control your tongue you are perfect. So you can tell how near perfection you are reaching, and it is God's will that we should all be made perfect. He is able to prevent us from falling and present us faultless before his throne, and that is his intention. He wants to make all of you perfect. My wife has tremendous faith, but there is one thing I teach that she finds very difficult to believe. She comes to the very edge of doubt when I say this, and it is when I tell her that one day her husband will be perfect. For some reason she finds this very hard to accept. I know what she would say: "If I base my faith on experience, I can't believe it, but I'll try and base it on the Word of God."

She is trying very hard! I have to believe that my wife will one day be perfect too. That is God's intention. He is able to complete a good work that he has begun in all of us, but it is easier for me to believe that she will be perfect one day than for her to believe that I will be.

That, then, is God's intention, so how do you measure your progress in holiness? Well, here is the ready gauge. If anybody doesn't say the wrong thing ever, they are perfect. They have reached Christian maturity. Do you never say the wrong thing? Who can say that? I certainly can't. That is the significance of your tongue. It is the spiritual measure of your Christian progress.

Not long ago, I went to the Iron Gorge, up in Shropshire, where there is a huge cast iron bridge over the River Severn, the first cast iron bridge ever made. There were stocks of coal and iron ore there, so that is where the Industrial Revolution began. But I wanted particularly to go to a village nearby called Madeley. I wanted to see the grave of a man at whose funeral John Wesley preached and took the text, "Mark the perfect man". A man who never said the wrong thing, his name was Fletcher. He was a Frenchman, and he was born on the shores of Lake Geneva. His name there had been Flechere, but he came as an immigrant to England, changed his name to Fletcher, which is the English version, and he became a Methodist preacher under John Wesley. Wesley said he was the one man who persuaded him that perfection was possible on earth by the grace of God.

He is buried in the little churchyard outside the parish church at Madeley. His tomb is above ground and it is all made of cast iron. His life story is in raised cast iron letters. Still they talk about him, though he died in the eighteenth century – Fletcher of Madeley. Wesley had chosen him to be his successor and to take over Methodism, but Fletcher died first and he never came into that position. On his grave it said "the perfect man" for he could control his tongue perfectly. An old hymn has the line: *Take my lips and let them be filled with messages from thee*. It is really a prayer that we may have total control of our tongues. Anyone who never says the wrong thing is perfect, and that is because if you can control that part of your body, you can control every other part, because that is the most difficult part to control.

James moves on to the size of the tongue – the extraordinary difference between its size and its influence. He talks about a bridle put in the mouth of a horse. It goes in the gap between its front and back teeth. There is a gap either side, and when you are harnessing a horse you get the bit in that gap, and because it has been broken in you can control the whole horse through that little bit of metal in the gap in its teeth. When I worked on a farm, indeed when I was only ten years old, we had two huge Shire carthorses. They are huge, and as a little boy I was awed by their size, yet, I would be left in charge of a hay-bogey with a stack, a pike of hay, and I would have the reins of this huge horse. The slightest pull on one side or the other and the horse would turn and the bogey would follow. I was always amazed that as a young boy I could control that huge thing. It was because I had a little thing in his mouth that I could control, and I had the control of the whole horse. That is the tongue. It is a little thing in the mouth between your teeth, but if you can control that bit, you can control the whole body, just as I could control the whole horse.

Or take the rudder of a huge ship; it has always amazed me when I see a ship out of water, either in model form or sometimes in dry dock, and you see the size of the rudder. Compared to the whole hull it is nothing, yet I know that the pilot, just turning that rudder a little bit, turns the whole ship. A modern illustration of that would be the ailerons on an aircraft wing. Have you ever watched, as you come in to land, those little strips of flap at the back of the wings? One just goes up a little and you feel the whole plane lurch. It is just a little bit of metal, and yet it turns the whole plane. I recently flew in a 380, one of the big double-decker planes, and I know because I have flown in a 320, for example, in the cockpit with a pilot I know who is a Christian. I have watched him as we have taken off, and he was holding a little joystick about three inches tall, and that is all he has got. This is the new wireless sort, new way of controlling a plane – just a little joystick, and that is all he used to turn the whole plane. It was quite weird. That magnificent huge machine did his perfect will.

The tongue is like that. Its size is out of all proportion to what it can achieve and what it can do to other people. So James illustrates the matter of size by a horse's bridle or bit in its mouth, or by a rudder on a huge ship, or by a forest fire. I have only once in my life experienced the horror of a forest fire – in South Australia. There was a high wind, and the flames were leaping from one tree to another. Since most of the trees were eucalyptus, full of flammable oil, you could see the flames rushing from one tree to another. In fact, the cars were being driven away from the flames at seventy miles an hour, because the flames were travelling at sixty. A tiny spark can start a forest fire, whether deliberately or not, and cause death and destruction. That is what the tongue is like – a fire which is tiny, but can set off a conflagration that will destroy many. James even goes so far as to say that the tongue is set on fire by hell. It is a demonic thing. The devil uses the tongue more than anything else to damage the social scene in which we live.

There was a lady in France who went to confession, and she told the priest, "I'm afraid I've been a gossip and I've been gossiping in this village for years."

The priest said, "Then you must do penance."

"Oh," she replied, "I'll do anything if I can be forgiven."

He said, "Well you must do these things. First of all, I want you to go and pluck two chickens and bring all the feathers to me in a bag," which she did.

She said, "Is that enough penance?"

"No, there's a second thing. You must now walk down the village street and take handfuls of feathers out of the bag and throw them up into the wind. When you have emptied the bag, come back."

When she came back, she said, "Is that enough penance?"

"No," he said, "There's a third thing."

"What's that?"

"This is all you need to do: now go and pick them all up."

She said, "But I'll never be able to find them all! They've blown away in the wind."

He replied, "That's what your gossip has been like. You can't ever get it back. It's gone! You've filled the village with your gossip, with your rumours."

A lady on a bus was overheard saying to another lady sitting next to her – about a third lady they both knew – "I don't like her, and from all I've said about her I never will," which was honest at least! We have all been guilty of gossip, and gossip is mentioned in many places in the Bible. It is a deadly thing. There are three questions to ask before you say anything about anyone else: is it true, is it kind, and is it necessary? If you ask those three things before you say anything about anyone else, you will find yourself controlling your tongue. One of the greatest philosophers said, "If everyone in the world knew what everyone had said about everybody else, there wouldn't be four friends left in the world." That may sound cynical, but you and I know there is an element of truth in it.

James moves on from the stubbornness of the tongue. There is something in the tongue that is wild, that cannot be tamed. He says, "Every other animal seems to be able to be tamed; the tongue, no." We know that even killer whales have been tamed; all kinds of animals have been tamed. When I was young, I went out of sheer curiosity to see a flea circus. Have you ever seen a flea circus? I didn't think you could train fleas, yet I watched as those fleas hauled little chariots around, walked on tightropes balancing weights, carrying burdens, doing all kinds of things. But then, there were plenty of fleas in those days to train. There are not so many now – they are quite rare – but fancy training a flea! Did you know that a worm can be trained and tamed? God did that. You find in the book of Jonah that God told a whale what to do and told a worm what to do. Which was the bigger miracle? Don't go by size. The larger miracle is telling a worm what to do. I have not seen a worm circus yet. Every kind of creature has been tamed, except the tongue.

Finally he mentions the schizophrenia of the tongue – a forked tongue. Snakes have a forked tongue, and James says our tongues are sometimes forked. We can bless people and we can curse people with the same tongue. We praise God and we criticise people. We can say nice things and nasty things with the same organ. That is the most unnatural thing about the tongue. In fact, James says that nature never has such contradictory or inconsistent behaviour. Human nature does; nature does not. There is no such thing in nature as inconsistency, and he illustrates this in two ways. The first is a spring of water. In Israel there are two kinds of spring. Some are full of salt. They come through natural salt deposits in the earth and they are foul to the taste, but good for your health if you bathe in them. So there are special places such as Tiberias, for example, where people came from all over to bathe in the spring water. Today in England you can go to Bath. I don't recommend drinking the water in Bath or Harrogate, though. It tastes pretty horrid, but it comes out like that. You don't expect fresh water, clean water, out of such a spring. Nature will be one or the other, never both.

Likewise trees – can a fig tree produce olives? Of course it can't. A fruit tree produces its own kind of fruit and you don't expect it to produce anything else. Yet here we are, our tongues can do what nature cannot do. Human nature can be schizophrenic. We can bless and curse with the same tongue. It is an extraordinary contradiction. So that is James's last point about this: possible in human nature, but not possible in nature itself. We are the exception to nature. We can do things that nature can't. We should not be able to, but we do it.

So here we have been given tongues by God to use, to praise and bless him, and to bless other people. One of the things we shall be judged on in the great Day of judgement is every *idle* word. I suppose we might translate that word of Jesus every *casual* word because it is what we say when we are not prepared, when we are just speaking off the cuff. We are usually careful when giving prepared words, but it is what we say when we are off our guard, when we are not careful. So Jesus said it is for every careless word that we shall be judged. Quite frankly, that means most of us may not have committed any other sin, but sins of speech are enough. They are set on fire by hell and they can take us to hell. No wonder James says "Don't be many teachers", because we have a strong temptation to tell people things that are not true.

I think of my interpretation of James 2. I trembled before I gave that to you because I was giving you an interpretation and an application of faith and works which the majority of evangelicals would not agree with. I had to go to the Lord before I conveyed that to you. In terms of written teaching, I think that today James would say "Don't be many writers", because when you write you are teaching in a very permanent way that will go far beyond your own voice and will influence many people. I know there are many Christians with an ambition to be a writer. They send me their manuscripts regularly. They want me to read them, correct them, commend them, find a publisher for them.

Quite honestly I never wanted or intended to write a single book. I loathed the idea. I thought it was the last example of egotism, and I just said when publishers demanded a book, "Sorry, I'm not a writer. I'm not writing." Then one day I was asking the Lord how I could share the burdens of my heart on a wider, more effective scale, and he took me to Jeremiah 30:2 – "'Write everything in a book that I've told you,' says the Lord." I wrote my first book out of obedience. I have written over thirty now, and they have all been out of sheer obedience.

So don't be many writers either, because they will face the same stricter judgement. I believe there are too many books that have not been ordered by God but have been an ambition for someone to get something off their chest. So if you are considering that you would love to write a book, then I would say please don't unless you have to, unless God says he wants you to do so. We would all love to be an influence on other people, but don't unless you can't help it. That is my final word on this part of the letter of James.

8
COMPETITION AND CO-OPERATION

Read James 3:13–18

A. DEMONSTRATING WISDOM (13)
    1. What you are – good lives
    2. What you do – good deeds
B. DESCRIBING WISDOM (14-16)
    1. False
        a. Its OPERATION
          i. Envy – putting others down
          ii. Ambition – pushing self up
        b. Its ORIGIN
          i. World ii. Flesh iii. Devil
        c. Its OUTCOME
          i. Disruption   ii. Depravity
    2. True
        a. Its ORIGIN
          i. Heaven ii. Spirit iii. God
        b. Its OPERATION
          i. Pure v. Evasive
          ii. Peaceable v. Aggressive
          iii. Considerate v. Thoughtless
          iv. Merciful v. Judgemental
          v. Beneficial v. Harmful
          vi. Impartial v. Biased
          vii. Sincere v. hypocritical
        c. Its OUTCOME
          i. Sow in peace
          ii. Harvest of righteousness

The Bible is full of wisdom. Some of the books are actually called wisdom literature. Proverbs is a book of wisdom. Ecclesiastes is a book of wisdom. Then there are people in the Bible who are known as people of great wisdom, and in the Old Testament the best example is Solomon, as we noticed in our study of James 1:2–18.

I have come to realise that Solomon was not the wisest man in the Bible. For one thing he had 700 mothers-in-law. Would you call that wise? He had 300 mistresses as well as his 700 wives. Solomon had wisdom for everybody else but himself. He was an example of a man who did not listen to his own teaching, but gave wise teaching to everybody else. Therefore he will be responsible to God for that stricter judgement.

The Jews have always put a tremendous emphasis on wisdom. Every synagogue hopes to have a rabbi who is wise, and not just wise but understanding. That is an important word. We are still thinking about teachers here. We have talked about the tool they use, their tongue, but now we are thinking about the qualification they need to be a teacher, which is summed up in those two words: wise and understanding. People will only go to someone with a problem if they feel he will understand as well as give them wisdom. The two go together and are almost synonymous. In Deuteronomy and in Proverbs both are mentioned in the same breath: "Whoever is wise and understanding...."

What is meant by that word "wise"? There are two sorts of wisdom we are going to realise: worldly wisdom and heavenly wisdom. One is the wisdom that comes to humans naturally and the other is wisdom that comes supernaturally. We will look at that in detail in a moment.

Jews admire wise men, holding them in high esteem. After all, it was wise men who came to find Jesus as a baby. I once saw a poster outside a church: "Wise Men Still Seek Jesus."

It was their Christmas message and I thought it was better than some messages I have seen outside church. I once put outside our church: "Danger – God at Work" in big red letters and it was the very week that a building contractor came to repair the outside of the church building. He wouldn't put his ladders up the building until I took the poster down.

What is the connection here with the verses we looked at above? Quite simply, you cannot be a teacher of others unless you are wise and understanding yourself. The first thing to say to anybody who thinks they are is: do you demonstrate wisdom? Before you declare it or describe it, you need to demonstrate it. You need to show someone that you are wise and understanding before you try and teach them anything. "Show and tell" is the phrase that is used in many primary schools. Children bring things to show the teacher and then tell them about it. That has always been the approach of the kingdom. Show them first, then tell them; demonstrate before you describe. It is the first qualification. Example must come before explanation. That is a very basic principle in the Bible, not just in wisdom.

But it is in wisdom, and how do you show people your wisdom? In two ways: in what you are, and in what you do. You judge wisdom in other people by these two vital tests: are they living good lives, and are they doing good deeds? As one cynical comment had it about a certain preacher, "What you are is so loud that I cannot hear what you say," which was quite a devastating assessment. In other words, you show the wisdom by how you handle your own affairs, and you do that first before you try and teach anybody else. Wise men are those who follow their own advice and live good lives. If they live good lives, that will inevitably lead to the second part of the demonstration of their wisdom: that they do good deeds, and they will do them in the humility that comes from wisdom. In other words, humility is one of the marks of the way they do good deeds – not boastfully.

I have a vivid recollection of when I was a little boy of about nine and a local doctor was chairing a missionary meeting in our church. I remember him announcing the collection, and then he put his hand in his pocket, pulled out a cheque book, opened it carefully in front of us, wrote out a sizeable cheque, told us how much it was for and then put it in the collection plate. That left an abiding memory in my mind. I thought, "Here is a man whose good deeds are not done in humility." He used even his giving to show off to a lot of people. Good deeds should be done in humility and meekness. Of course Jesus and Moses were noted for their meekness. It is not weakness. It is to do things quietly; to do good deeds without expecting any return, even in reputation. All this will show what we think of ourselves, and prove our wisdom, prove it to others and commend it to them. This is very simple but terribly important. Demonstrate wisdom before you claim to be wise.

The next part of the passage describes wisdom. There is the wisdom that is human, and the wisdom that is heavenly, and there is a huge difference between them. There are plenty of "wise" people in the world who are clever and they can give good advice within their sphere of knowledge and experience – but theirs is human wisdom, not the kind of wisdom that Christian teachers need, which is heavenly wisdom. We are going to see in these five remaining verses of James 3 the contrast between human wisdom and heavenly wisdom, or as James describes it, false wisdom and true wisdom. I want to say a little about this word "true". The words translated "true" and "real" are the same words in Greek and Hebrew. "The truth will set you free," said Jesus. He was saying that reality will set you free, a real understanding of the real situation. A truthful understanding of yourself and of God will set you free.

Let us look first at false human wisdom. It can be fatally flawed and, therefore, fatally misleading if it is in any way flawed by its motivation. We need to look at the contrast between these two kinds of wisdom at their origin – where they come from, the way they operate, and finally, the outcome of following these two kinds of wisdom. It is not quite the same order in both of them, and James begins with the way false human wisdom operates. He looks at the motives that can get mixed up behind it. One motive is envy and the other is ambition. These two wrong motivations can spoil human wisdom. One is a wrong attitude to other people, and one is a wrong attitude to themselves. If wisdom involves pulling others down and pushing self up, then it will be misleading. It will be unreal eventually. If there is envy of others, this "wisdom" will be setting itself over against them and wanting to make them less than they are, and will be pushing its own "wisdom" and wanting to make that more than it is. This can lead to contempt for others and pride and arrogance in oneself. So the first thing to look at is the motivation: what is driving someone to be wise in worldly wisdom? Is it that they are envious of other people? Is it that they are proud and pushing themselves? Why are they wise? Why are they offering their wisdom to other people? That is the first thing that is said about the false wisdom. Any trace of pulling others down and pushing self up means that it is human wisdom and not the wisdom that is needed in teachers.

Now let us look at its *origin*. Where does it come from, this human wisdom? There is an awful lot of human wisdom being offered to us in the mass media. Where does that come from? From three very familiar sources. It is coming from the world. It is accumulated "wisdom" of the ages, passed on from parent to child. It is coming out of this world, and therefore it is coming from below. If we are not careful that is where we pick up our wisdom – passed on in schools and universities and often mistaken for knowledge. Such "knowledge" itself may be accurate and good, but there is a lack of wisdom there.

The Bible is not a book to make you clever, rich or famous. If you want those things you need the wisdom of the world. You get plenty of that wisdom if you make your ambitions known. I remember a book being published years ago entitled *How to Win Friends and Influence People*. That was the kind of book that sold in millions around World War II and it was offering worldly wisdom that had been gained by people over the years. The world is not the best place to get your wisdom from. I have sometimes thought of writing a book *How to Lose Friends and Influence People* because I know more about that now!

The second source is your flesh – yourself, your own common sense, your own thinking, your own ideas. In the Bible, the flesh refers to your unredeemed fallen nature, so once again you are getting your wisdom from a faulty source. You are getting it from yourself, and "flesh" in scripture is easily spelled backwards "s-e-l-f" dropping the "h". The third, and the most dangerous source of all, is the worldly wisdom that comes from the devil. After all, he is the god of this world, the ruler of this world, the prince of this world. Don't ever underestimate the devil. He is in charge of our world or, as John says in his letter: "We know that we are of God, but the whole world lies in the grip of the evil one." Ultimately, worldly wisdom comes from the devil, and that is a dangerous source, not to be encouraged.

So worldly wisdom does not come from God, it comes from the world, the flesh, or the devil, or all three, and therefore is suspect, for these are the very three things that Christians have renounced. Sometimes at their baptism people are asked, "Do you renounce the world, the flesh and the devil?" Are you cutting yourself off from those three sources of worldly wisdom, because they are the three things that Jesus came to redeem you from – to rescue you from?

Now let us turn to look at the *outcome* of worldly wisdom. What happens when you follow such wisdom, which is false and will ultimately lead you astray? If there is envy in it, if there is selfish ambition in it, then as sure as anything it is going to lead to troubles – two in particular. The first thing it leads into is disruption or disorder. It will divide people. It will bring confusion among them. It will even bring chaos among them. Mentally they will begin to lose grip of the situation. The second thing that follows from that: when you lose your mental grip, you lose your moral grip, and every kind of debauchery will come in, every kind of depravity. This is the inevitable result of getting your wisdom from the wrong sources.

How is it that the human race is totally unable to solve the problems of war? With all our worldly wisdom we are quite unable to deal with war, which we all agree is bad for us and wrong. Yet we just do not seem able at all to stop wars. I talk about the last war as 1939–1945. What a silly way to talk! There have been at least 36 international wars since 1945, to say nothing of all the civil wars. We change our government regularly in the hope that they will have the wisdom to settle things and make them good and happy for us, and as one prime minister cynically said of a general election: "Means one lot of sinners out and another lot in." We very quickly find they do not have the wisdom that they need to solve our real problems, because they are relying on this false wisdom. Disruption, disharmony and depravity inevitably follow. Things start out well, and it sounds sensible and wise and good. I can remember my first funeral in the Shetland Islands. I was very surprised at the number of men who came to the funeral, men I had never seen in church. We laid the brother's body in the earth and then all these men filed past and threw something into the grave. I never saw what it was, and I inquired afterwards, "Who were all these men?" They said, "They're all the freemasons of the local lodge." I knew nothing about freemasonry at that stage. I found that most of the men in Shetland, when they came back out of the army, navy and air force after World War II, missed the kind of brotherhood of the forces. They found the alternative in the local lodge, and they joined up and they found it was a great time of male company. They advised me very strongly, "If you want to succeed, you'd be very wise to join the freemasons." They told me all the advantages I would have. I didn't know then what I have learned since, but there were churches of my denomination in London, for example, that would not call me to be a minister until I had joined the lodge and was a freemason. They all sounded so sensible and so wise. They did everything they could to persuade me it was an innocent body, that it did good to widows and orphans and that it was a good thing. It sounded so sensible to me in that time. I nearly joined, but thank God I didn't. It all sounded so wise.

I remember being advised very strongly by a man in finance to put what savings I had into an overseas bank where I would be protected from tax. He put a very strong, sensible case to me to look after my money in this way with an offshore bank account. It all sounded so wise. From his point of view he was really trying to help me, but I didn't do it and I thank God that something kept me from doing it. Worldly wisdom can sound very convincing, very persuasive, but it is coming from the wrong source. Thank God that James has told us where it comes from and how to be careful about the advice you receive.

That is its outcome, but James devotes most attention to its operation and then about true wisdom but, before he can tell us even that, he must look at the origin of true wisdom.

It does not come from the world. It does not come from the flesh. It does not come from the devil, it comes from above. There is just that simple word: *above*. Its origin is heaven. No-one will ever be wise as God counts wise until their wisdom comes from above and not below. Secondly, it comes from the Spirit. It is spiritual wisdom. It is a gift of the Holy Spirit. It is a word of wisdom sometimes. The Holy Spirit can give you just one word that is so wise that it just releases the situation.

Let me give you an example of a word of wisdom. Forgive me being personal, but it is more real when you do that. I was preaching in east London, and after I had finished and most of the people had gone, a lovely little couple came up to me. They said, "David, you've got to help us." I don't respond readily to people who say you've got to do something, but nevertheless I said, "Why? What's the matter?" They said, "If you don't help us, we are getting divorced." I said, "How long have you been married?" They said, "Three months." I thought, "Help, what's going wrong here?" So I asked them, "Well, tell me how you met." They said, "We met in prison." She was a prison visitor and they foolishly sent her to a man's prison. That was a mistake if ever there was one. She should have been sent to a women's prison, but the inevitable happened. She met a young man who had committed a serious crime and was in for some time. She was a Christian, and she led this young man to Christ. There is no question about it, he really was converted, and they were both real Christians, yet after three months they were going to get divorced if I didn't do something about it. I said, "Well, what went wrong?" They said, "Everything." They said that, because she counselled him, inevitably they became attracted and fell for each other. When the time finally came for him to be discharged from jail, he then told her that he had no relatives and no friends on the outside, and therefore no-one to go to – no job, no home, nothing. She was twenty-seven and had a flat, and was virtually an orphan, with no family of her own. He then said, "You must realise that I've fallen for you," and she said, "Well, you must know that's returned; it's reciprocal, I'm in love with you." They thought, since they were both Christians, the best thing to do was to get married as soon as they could and live together in her apartment, which they did. As soon as he was released, they went to a register office and got married, but they had never seen each other outside a prison cell and therefore knew next to nothing about one another. When they married and moved in together, into her flat, they discovered they were totally different to the point of incompatibility. Quite simply, she had been brought up in a middle-class background where you were tidy, in a home with lace curtains, where when you undressed at night you carefully folded your clothes or put them away in the drawer. She ate with a knife and fork and spoon. He did none of those things. He ate with his fingers. After all, they were made before knives and forks, weren't they? At night when he got undressed, he simply pulled his clothes off and left them on the floor at the side of the bed. In the morning he would put his feet inside his trousers and pull them up. After three months they couldn't stand each other and said, "We've made the most terrible mistake. We should never have married." They made the same mistake as some other Christian couples, thinking if you are both Christians everything is going to be all right – and it wasn't. They got on each other's nerves and had said, "We're going to get divorced. We've come to that point. We should admit we made the biggest mistake of our lives and that's it."

I had a limited amount of time before I had to go home. It sounded as if they needed six months' counselling, but I said, "Holy Spirit, please give me a word of wisdom," and he did. I said, "Now listen carefully. This is what the Holy

Spirit wants you to do. You should do "week on, week off", both of you. The first week you both live the same way that she lives, and you (the husband) learn to fold your clothes; learn to eat with a knife and fork. The next week it is your week off, and she has to do everything your way. She has to drop her clothes on the floor and eat with her fingers. You are to do week on, week off. They said, "That's so crazy, it's got to be of the Lord." I said, "That's all I can hear from him." She said, "Nothing else?" I said, "No—week on, week off. Those are the four words that come to me." They walked away.

I have never seen them again, but I have heard from them. I had the loveliest letter just six months later. The letter said, "Dear Mr Pawson, we have never been so happy." They both were writing and they just went on, saying, "We're just blissfully happy. We love each other and it's great living together...." and so on and so forth. I've still got the letter and it is the happiest letter you can imagine. I thought, "Now I've got the answer. I can write a book on marriage now, and I'm going to call it "Week On, Week Off", but I have never written that book, and I have never given anybody else that advice. It was a word of wisdom from the Holy Spirit for them and for no-one else, and it worked. Instead of months of counselling, a couple of minutes and God's heavenly wisdom for that couple was given. It comes from heaven. It is a gift of the Holy Spirit. Wisdom is one of his most precious gifts to people, and also therefore it comes from God himself. It is divine, and God is described in the New Testament as the "only wise God". His wisdom is the subject of many texts in your Bible.

There is the origin of true wisdom. Having seen that, let us turn to the *operation* of this amazing wisdom. I have used adjectives to describe this, but actually the Bible uses adverbs. The difference is that an adjective is static but an adverb is dynamic. Nevertheless, I have put them into adjectives so that you can understand them better. I have even put the opposite of each adjective to make it clearer what we are talking about. The first thing about this wisdom that is true is that it is *pure*. There are no hidden motives, no cards held close to the chest, everything is above board. There is no mixture of good and bad there. Everything else follows from this. The opposite of pure wisdom is to be evasive, ambiguous, shifty. That is the first way that you tell whether you are dealing with human or heavenly wisdom. There is nothing hidden, no guile, it is straightforward and open.

The second thing is that it is peaceable. There is no shouting, no raised voices or raised temperature. It is simply wisdom, simply wise and there is no argument about it. It is not aggressive. That would be the opposite of this lovely word *peaceable*. Some people give wisdom in an aggressive manner. They force it on you. They bully you into accepting their advice. The heavenly wisdom is not like that. It is peaceable, and when I told that young couple "Week on, week off" I did not shout at them. I did not say you have got to do this. It was the girl who said, "That's so crazy it's got to be of the Lord," and so they accepted it. I did not have to argue them into it. They recognised it as a word from God, they did it, and everything is hunky-dory as a result. "Blessed are the peacemakers," said Jesus. "Theirs is the kingdom of heaven."

Thirdly, heavenly wisdom is *considerate*. It considers other people's feelings, thoughts and character, background and interests. It is considerate, or to put it very simply, *heavenly wisdom is a good listener*. It listens, it does not just speak. It *considers* carefully. The opposite of considerate is *thoughtless*. You can invade other people's privacy and personality with thoughtless wisdom.

The fourth characteristic is that it is *submissive*. What do we mean by that? It means it is ready to give way. It does not stand so strongly on its own with wording that will not brook any other opinion. It is neither stubborn nor obstinate. Submissive, it is willing to give way to others, willing to yield.

Fifth, it is merciful to those who are opposed to what is being said or to those who are wrong and oppose it. Mercy is needed when there is opposition. The opposite is being judgmental. Being merciful gives the benefit of the doubt to people; being judgmental does not give any room for manoeuvring. "Merciful" means practical help, not just pity or sympathy.

Sixth, it is *beneficial*. It bears good fruit. It is not harmful. Heavenly wisdom is never harmful.

Seventh, it is *impartial*. It is objective. Too often advice and counsel is given in a subjective way, and the person giving it is involved emotionally. Heavenly wisdom has no self-interest in it. It is standing back from a situation and seeing it in true perspective. Therefore it does not need to be biased. Heavenly wisdom from above is never biased, never prejudiced.

Eighth, finally, it is *sincere*. We are back to where we started. It is pure, without guile – no hidden motives. The opposite of this would be *hypocritical*. Heavenly wisdom is never hypocritical. It is utterly sincere, through and through.

That is a lovely description of true wisdom, and you know now where it comes from. There are two examples in scripture of heavenly wisdom. Solomon is not one of them, because he never listened to his own advice. He wisely applied it to everybody else, but he himself married far too many people when God had only one girl for him, and she was number sixty-one. He made a song. I have a theory about Solomon's songs. The Bible says he wrote 1005 songs, and we only have about five of them in Scripture, some of them in the book of Psalms. So where did all the others go? God never published them. I think he wrote a song for every girl he married. I will check out my theory when I get to heaven, but I reckon he wrote a love song and sang it to each girl he married. We have that Song of Solomon in our Bible – one of the few books in the Bible that does not mention God or prayer or salvation or anything spiritual. It is a love song because that was the girl that God wanted for him.

Who then are the wisest men in the Old and the New Testament? The wisest man in the Old Testament is Moses. The wisest man in the New Testament is Jesus. In fact it says Jesus is our wisdom. The Holy Spirit when he gives that wisdom to us is really giving us something of Jesus, and we are going to react in the same way that Jesus reacted. He is our wisdom. Moses, the wisest man in the Old Testament, got his wisdom from the same place. One of the things that Jesus said was this: "The Father gives me what to say and how to say it." Did you ever notice that? Wisdom not only knows *what* to say, but *how* to say it. I think that is very important because you might have a word from the Lord for someone, but do let him tell you how to share it so that you do it his way. Plenty of people pass on, "I have a word from the Lord for you," but they don't do it in his way. Jesus said that; it is in John 12. "The Father tells me what to say and how to say it." How wise that is!

Let us look finally at the *outcome* of this heavenly wisdom. We looked at that with the false wisdom; now we look at that for the true wisdom. What kind of result comes from it? Here we have a picture taken from agriculture. It is a profoundly divine principle that whatever a man sows that will he also reap. Heavenly wisdom is sown in peace, and then it will be harvested in righteousness. He has used this picture of sowing and reaping because there is a lot of time between the two. A farmer sows in the knowledge that one day he will be reaping in that field the results of his sowing. In the same way, heavenly wisdom does not always produce the results we hope for immediately. It takes time, but it is sown in peace, not in anxiety or rushed; and harvested in righteousness. That means, quite simply, that heavenly wisdom in the long run produces better people; righteous people; holy people. Heavenly wisdom makes people better. I cannot put it more simply. That couple that I met are now better people as the result of wisdom from on high. It did not show until six months later (or I didn't know until six months later), but the result of those four little words "week on, week off" produced a harvest of righteousness. There is a marriage that was saved and will not end in divorce, but has brought great joy to them and to everybody else who knows them.

Now this is why I headed this section *Competition and Co-operation*, because worldly wisdom, human wisdom, leads to a competitive society. The advice you give tends to divide rather than unite, whereas heavenly wisdom has the opposite effect – it brings people together. It resolves differences, and how much it is needed in Christian circles. If your church is led by people with nothing but human wisdom, it will not be long before you have division and even depravity among you. Pray to God for your leaders that they will pray for heavenly wisdom.

We are actually right back at the start of this letter of James. Right in the first chapter he had said this: "Does any of you lack wisdom?" All you have got to do is ask for it. Pray for it, and it will be yours. What a contrast to all the prayers of the world – many pray for health, for safety, and for all kinds of things. You don't often hear the world pray for wisdom, do you? They pray for all they think they need, and the one thing they really do need is theirs for the asking: it is wisdom and understanding. Happy is the fellowship that has wise leaders who have prayed for wisdom.

9
HOSTILITY AND HARMONY

Read James 4:1–12

A. CAUSE (1-6) – why things go wrong
    1. Human envy (1-3)
       a. Don't get – what we want
       b. Don't ask – right person
       c. Don't receive – wrong motive
    2. Divine enmity (4-6)
       a. Friend of world is enemy of God
       b. Spirit within us tends to envy
       c. God opposes the proud,
         gives grace to the humble

B. CURE (7-12) how to put things right
    1. Relationship with heavenly Father
      (7-10) – what to do
       a. Draw near to God and he
         will draw near to you
       b. Resist the devil and he
         will flee from you
       c. Humble yourself and
         God will lift you up
    2. Relationship with earthly brothers
      (11-12) – what not to do
       a. Their judge
       b. Their lawgiver
       c. Only Lawgiver and Judge

There is a lot of good practical advice in this passage. James is assuming that among believers there will be quarrels and conflicts. The reason is very simple: when we come to Christ, we are not perfect immediately. One day you will be, but the church is made up of imperfect people, so wherever people live together in community, sooner or later there will be conflict and arguments and quarrels, even among believers. Therefore we should expect this and certainly not leave the church because there are quarrels in it. You may be part of the quarrel in any case.

Where do these conflicts come from? We must root them out by identifying the root cause. Running through this whole section there is one note which I want to highlight so that we have it in the back of our minds, namely the pursuit of pleasure. We live in a world where this is a major part of life. Most people in our world are pursuing pleasure of one kind or another, and if we are not careful we pick that up ourselves and this is where the trouble starts.

The cause of quarrels, discord and disharmony lies within ourselves. There are desires at war within, and most external quarrels are a projection of a struggle inside that we are reading into other people. James identifies the conflict within and teaches us that it is the root cause even of war. The root cause is that we don't get what we want. We all have desires in us for things, and when we don't get them that creates conflict inside. With some people their conflict is due to the fact that they have never got their own way, but getting things is in James's mind here. We don't get it, and the result is we fight for it. A lot of human conflicts are due, quite simply, to the fact that people do not get what they want and are striving and fighting for it. This kind of thing, says James, can kill. Is he exaggerating? No! Envy is a killer. It was actually responsible for the first murder in human history and the worst murder in human history. Cain killed Abel out of jealousy, out of envy, and it was for envy that they nailed Christ to the cross. Envy is a deadly poison.

When you want something that somebody else has and that you have not got, it can ultimately lead you to violence, but it is basically coveting. Two opposite things in scripture are coveting and contentment, and you can never have both. We choose between them. You are either content with what you have got, or you are coveting what somebody else has. If your heart is covetous you are certainly not content with what you have. That is where it all starts. Notice that it is what we want, rather than what we need. Practical wisdom is to discern between your needs and your wants.

When a little boy was reciting the twenty-third Psalm, he said, "The Lord's my shepherd; that's all I want." He got the real meaning of "want" there. To say, "I shall not want" means that I am content with what I have. I shall not want what I have not got. God is providing for what I need, and what more do I need than that? H. G. Wells wrote a famous book entitled *The History of Mr Polly*. In the book he says, "Mr Polly was not so much a human being as a civil war." That is a profound remark and it applies to most of us, but our battle, of which other people may not be aware, is going on inside. It is the battle, says James, between what we have and what we want. That tension builds up.

The next thing James says is that you are not asking the right person for what you want – you should be asking God because everything is his. If you want something, then ask God. I love that phrase in Psalm 50 where God says, "If I were hungry, I wouldn't tell you." That tells you something about God. He has got everything. The next verse is, "The cattle on a thousand hills are mine, and all the silver and the gold is mine," says the Lord. So why don't you ask him instead of coveting and wanting something from someone else? Go to the one who could give it to you. In fact God himself is the only real source of satisfaction.

But people say, "I went to God, and I didn't get what I wanted." James says that there is a simple answer to that, too: you didn't get what you wanted from God because you asked with the wrong motive. You only wanted what you were asking for to spend on your own pleasure. In other words, unanswered prayer is often due to being selfish in what you asked. That tells us something about prayer life that is very important to know. "Lord, please ... I'd love a Rolls Royce." "No!" That is an answered prayer. You got the answer from God. We often confuse un-replied prayer with unanswered prayer. When people say they have a problem about unanswered prayer, they don't mean that God didn't reply, they simply mean he did not do what they wanted. We ask for the wrong motive. Try asking God for things that are not for your pleasure. Instead of asking for your safety, your health, your comfort, and your everything else, ask for something for somebody else. That is always an acceptable prayer to God. It has not got self in it.

Here is James's analysis of why we project our own troubles on to other people. We don't get what we want. We don't ask the right person for it, and if we do, we don't get the answer that we want because we have selfish motives behind it. We are asking for our own sake and our pleasure. Now all this is characteristic of the world in which we live. It is characteristic of worldly people's prayer lives, too. When do they pray? When they are likely to lose their pleasure, likely to lose their health, likely to lose their safety. Most people pray when their pleasure is affected in some way and threatened. So they pray, "Don't let it happen, Lord." That is quite a selfish prayer when you think about it.

Deep down, then, human envy is the ultimate cause of conflict within us, which then becomes the conflict outside us, and this even extends to simply getting our own way. If we don't get that, it sets up conflict, and sooner or later that will divide us from other people.

There is another factor to it all, and a very important one. That is divine enmity. That goes along with human envy. We live in a world that is godless, a world that is actually god-hating. People say, "Oh no; I can't believe that about our nice neighbours." Just a minute – you try telling them the truth about God. Try telling them the truth about themselves. You will very quickly realise we live in a world that hates God as he really is: the Holy One of Israel, God as he has revealed himself to be. The world does not want that kind of God. The world hates being reminded of that kind of God. The world hates being reminded that that God will judge every human being for how they have lived. So without realising it you find yourself on the side of those who hate God. Here we are treading on very delicate thin ice, but in fact James says quite simply that you cannot be a friend of the world or you are an enemy of God. If you are a friend of God, then the world is your enemy. We must face this.

What about John 3:16, the favourite verse of many Christians: "For God so loved the world...." So people say, "Well, shouldn't we love the world? If God does, shouldn't we?" But if you turn to the first letter of John, you will find an extraordinary statement. The same John who wrote in John 3:16 that God loved the world, says this: "Do not love the world or anything in the world. If anyone loves the world, the love of the Father is not in him. For everything in the world – the cravings of sinful man, the lust of his eyes and the boasting of what he has and does – comes not from the Father but from the world." Just ask yourself and your unbelieving neighbours, what they boast about, or to put it simply, what they are proud of. You will find a little list of what they are proud of – their achievements, their possessions, their appearance. Make a list of the things that they are happy to tell you about. It is an extraordinary list, and, says John the apostle, it is safe for God to love the world, but it is not safe for you. These are alien things to the true son of God. John is using the same word for love and the same word for world as in John 3:16. He is telling us not to do what God does because God does not get contaminated. We do, and the more friends we have in the world, the more we are likely to be like them. Christians have got to be on their guard. Yes, by all means have personal relationships with unbelievers, especially if you are trying to win them for the Lord, but friendship with the world is a different matter. You always have the reservation: I don't want the things that you want, and therefore I can never get as excited as you about your achievements and your appearance and your possessions. That is the point at which you reveal that you are different.

So the divine enmity is another factor in this situation of living in the world but not being of it. It is a tension that every Christian knows because one of the most powerful pressures on us is to be acceptable to people, not to be an enemy of people. There is something in us that wants to be accepted and wants to be well thought of. That is where the snare lies. It is a simple choice. You cannot have both. The world is godless.

There was an opinion poll about which nation in the world is the most godless. They came up with the finding that Britain is the second most godless country in the world. They found that Japan was the most godless – not the least religious, but the most godless, in other words where people live their ordinary lives without reference to God. They came to the conclusion that Japan was number one and Britain was number two. I am sure you are aware of how many people from overseas have come to this country thinking they were coming to a Christian country and then were shocked to find out what we are really like. It is not that we don't have churches everywhere. It is not that we are not religious. It is simply that most of us live most of our lives as if God were not there. In the Bible it is the man who says in his heart "There is no God" who is called a fool. Practical atheism is more serious than theoretical atheism.

Now we come to v. 5. I use the New International Version (NIV) and jokingly I say it is the "Nearly Infallible Version". Here is a verse where it is not infallible, and there are a number of verses in James where NIV has got it wrong. I showed that the punctuation in James 2 in the NIV has it wrong, and this verse has it very wrong: "Or do you think scripture says without reason that the spirit he caused to live in us envies intensely? But he gives us more grace." What on earth does that mean? In fact, the NIV has given you two alternative translations at the bottom of the page. One is: "that God jealously longs for the spirit that he made to live in us"; or, "that the spirit he calls to live in us longs jealously." That third translation is getting near it.

The NIV often gets envy and jealousy mixed up, and that is a tragedy. In Romans 11 Paul says, win the Jews by making them jealous, but if you change that word to envy as NIV does, it alters the whole thing. Do you know the difference between envy and jealousy? If I meet somebody whose wife I prefer to mine, that would be envy (I have not done so yet). If I did, I would be envious. If somebody runs away with my wife, I would be jealous. Do you see the difference? Envy is what you feel towards somebody else's possession. Jealousy is what you feel towards your own, so NIV has got it seriously wrong here in translating it "envy". It should be jealousy. What this verse is saying is that scripture tells us that the Spirit God has caused to live within us is jealous, and thank God that he is jealous! He is not envious. He could not be envious because everything is his anyway. What would God envy in your life? Nothing; it is all his, but he

153

can be terribly jealous. That means the kind of anger that is aroused when somebody runs off with his possessions. This is why right the way through scripture, God is jealous. He is jealous for his people, jealous for his name, for what he has, and he cannot bear others to run away with what belongs to him. Therefore, in the Old Testament, God was jealous for Israel. If any false gods got hold of them, God was angry. He was jealous. Those are my people! You shouldn't have them! We will win Jews by making them jealous – not by making them envious of what we have, but by making them jealous for what they already have but do not acknowledge. Make them jealous of the scriptures – not ours, theirs; their saviour, their Messiah. That is a very different approach.

The spirit within us is jealous, and here we have a very strong statement that began in v. 4, telling them they are adulterous people. That is not the actual word used. The word is "you adulteresses". That is a very important point. It is a female word. You are the bride of Christ and when the world runs off with you, Christ is jealous. He is bound to be. You belong to him. In the Old Testament, prophets again and again accused Israel of being an adulteress because God was her husband and they were running after other gods and their God is jealous.

Now I shall tell you something else that I can't forgo mentioning. Always in scripture God is male. He is king of the universe, not queen. He is husband of Israel. He is never the wife of Israel. He is Father from beginning to end of scripture, never mother. Occasionally there are statements that like a mother he cares for his children, but there is not a single statement in the whole of the Bible that he *is* a mother. Even the prayers on the BBC are now praying to God as mother. We live in a day when under the name of equality between male and female – equality means *identity* and therefore the same role and the same responsibility – a woman can do or a man can do and we must get rid of all discrimination on gender. Well I do not apologise for writing a book entitled *Leadership is Male*, and it runs right against political correctness, but I believe God always calls himself a male and his people female. Christians are the bride of Christ, not the bridegroom. Christ is the bridegroom. He is the male, and we in that sense are his female—the bride of Christ. It is always the Lord's people that are portrayed in female metaphors and God and Christ are portrayed in male metaphors.

That is a very important point, but it is no longer popular to say so. Here if you are a friend of the world you will say that women can do the same things as men and they are equal and therefore identical. It is going right against the Creator who made male and female and made them for different roles and different responsibilities. All this is very relevant because females are in ministry and this has been the big issue for the last twenty-five years. There are women bishops in some churches, so the church itself is departing from the Word of God in this. I believe that firmly, but have been in trouble for saying so, for saying things that thirty years ago I could have said freely, but not now. Now we are into this equality identity thinking of the secular age. I just throw that in because when we become friends of the world we are behaving like an adulterous wife and the husband will be jealous. The Holy Spirit within us will be jealous for us. We belong to the Lord.

Scripture says he has put this jealous spirit within us to guard us, and it adds "and he will give more grace" to keep it that way. It is all there in that verse, so you see there is a mistranslation in that verse. Don't let it upset you. No translation of scripture is infallible. There have been mistakes by translators in every translation. That is why it is good to compare translations. I have a book entitled *The*

New Testament in Twenty-Six Translations where I can look up and compare 26 versions. It is a great help, and they are now busy producing the Old Testament in 26 translations. The Book of Psalms has come out already.

So friendship with the world is enmity with God. The Spirit within us is jealous and God will give us more grace to be different from the world and to stand out from the world and say: I'm sorry, but my convictions are different, I've taken them from a different source.

The third thing is that God opposes the proud and exalts the humble. Therefore, when pride enters any human being for any reason, God will resist them. He is an enemy of pride, and proud people are those he brings low. You can see that in history. Proud dictators, proud rulers, are brought very low. The classic example in the Bible is Nebuchadnezzar. Read Daniel 4. It is the most amazing story of a man who became so proud he composed a new prayer. "Mine is the kingdom, the power and the glory, Amen." The Lord drove him mad, and he became so crazy, they locked him up in his own private zoo like an animal. For years he ate grass and his nails grew like eagle's talons. It is astonishing how he came to his senses, and finally lifted up his eyes to God and said, "God, I should have said 'Yours is the kingdom; yours is the power; yours is the glory.'" God gave him his sanity back again immediately.

God has humbled so many proud people through the ages. As soon as a man gets too big for his boots, as soon as he thinks he has it, or as soon as he thinks he is the great 'I Am', which is God's name, God has a way of bringing that man very low, humbling him. God loves to lift humble people up. God loves nobodies. That is why there are so many of them in the church. I am just quoting 1 Corinthians 1 where Paul says, "Look at you – not many noble, not many high-ups," and there aren't. There never are in church, because

God favours the humble. It does not mean he never saves a rich or powerful person, but it is always an exception to God. God's rule is that humble people are the important people. Nobodies are the ones he wants to bless and make into somebodies. All the way down the ages some of the outstanding Christians have come from nothing. When you read their life stories you wonder how they ever made it, but God chose them. Isn't that great news? If you are a nobody then God can lift you right up and make you a somebody for him. He has done that all along.

So that is where the conflicts arise. On the one hand there is human envy, and on the other hand divine enmity. Put the two together and you have a complete explanation as to why conflicts happen, but the important thing is the cure. The Bible not only gives us the cause of things, but also the cure for them. Plenty of people can identify a cause and discuss the world's problems and diagnose them, but to say this is the cure for them is something else. Most of us are good at analysing the problem. We are not so good at curing it, saying what should be done about it. Verses 7–12 are the cure for conflicts and quarrels, how to put things right, and the first basic thing is: put things right with God first, and then, secondly, with people.

Here we are given a series of three steps we can take which draw the right response from others. In vv. 7–10 we are told exactly what we need to do to put everything right, and what the response to that will be from the other side. In other words, the initiative is ours, and the response will be that of other people and that of the Father. We have eight aorist imperatives (as they are called by the Greek scholars), meaning eight commands to us to take the first step to put it right and to do something that will get a response that will solve the problem.

1. Draw near to God, and the result will be that he will draw near to you.

That is the first initiative and response mentioned here. James has already said to submit to God. Get the God angle right and the rest will follow.

2. Resist the devil and he will run away from us.

Have you ever tried that? This assumes that you believe there is a devil, and that he is a real person, and that it is possible to talk to him. One of the ways you can resist the devil is to talk to him and tell him. I know one Christian who said "Get the hell out of here" to the devil. That is not a bad place to send him. Martin Luther, when he was translating the Bible, had a real temptation from the enemy, and he took his inkwell and he threw it at the devil. In the room in the castle where this happened they will still show you the mark on the wall where the inkwell hit it. The devil does not have authority over you, particularly since your baptism. Throw your baptism at the devil. Tell him: "I am baptised, and since then you have no rights over me." That does not seem to occur to many Christians. Your baptism is crucial in your relationship to the Devil.

I must tell you about a friend of mine, a Baptist minister in the north of London. He and another boy were close friends for years while at school, but when they left school they drifted apart and lost contact. He was converted and became a Baptist minister, but his friend went the opposite way, got into real trouble and went rapidly downhill. By about twenty-four years of age his friend was desperate and contemplating suicide. Everything seemed to have gone wrong with his life. Then in desperation, before he committed suicide, he thought, "I wish I could get in touch with my friend from school, because I'm sure he would help me; nobody else will." He deliberately went to a spiritist medium in Bristol to consult the medium to see if she could tell him where his friend from schooldays was. He described his friend and the medium said, "Well, I can tell you what kind of house he lives in, but not the address." She described exactly this house in north London opposite a park full of trees, but she said: "I don't know the address. I do have to tell you that your friend from school is dead. I'll give you the date of his death." Well, he set off for London and he walked around north London for days, looking for the house. He found it and rang the bell, and was shattered when his friend from school came to the door. They were reunited, and the friend who was the Baptist minister led him to the Lord and got him on the road of salvation and changed his life. The friend said, "I got your house description from a spiritist medium, but she told me that you were dead and she gave me the date of your death." My friend said to him, "What date was that?" He replied, "Would you believe it? That was the date of my baptism!"

You don't realise how much baptism means to Satan. It means the same as the Red Sea meant to Pharaoh. Don't have a low view of baptism. It is not just a wet witness. It is a profound transaction between you and the Lord, and it is drowning Satan! Satan lost his authority over you the day you were baptised into the name of Jesus. Did you realise that? Remind the devil of your baptism and say, "You get out of here! You have no authority over me at all. I'm a baptised believer in the name of the Lord Jesus. That's who I belong to now."

Jesus resisted the devil when, through Peter, the devil tempted him not to go to the cross. Jesus said immediately, "Get behind me, Satan!" not "Get behind me, Peter." Jesus recognised who was in charge of Peter's tongue at that moment.

Resisting the devil involves speaking to him, addressing him in the name of Christ, telling him where he gets off. The result you will find, is that he runs away from you. He just gets out of it. Jesus himself resisted the devil with words of the Bible, and it says: "So Satan left him for a season." The devil came back again later, but he fled from Jesus, and this is the truth. You can resist the Devil and he will run from you. That is the second thing for you to do to cure quarrels and conflicts.

3. Humble yourselves, and God will lift you up.

We have already seen that God lifts up the humble and humbles the proud.

So there are three steps for us to take which will each draw the response we need to get out of this quarrelsome situation. It is amazing, but the initiative is ours. We have to take the first step in each of the three cases. A step towards God, a step against Satan, and a step against ourselves; those are the three relationships that we need to put right when we have got into quarrels and conflicts. Those three statements state things that are bound to happen. They are not just "try them out and maybe it'll improve the situation", but "do this and this will happen". They are promises in disguise that if we take this initiative we shall get the response. Only then, after you have done those three things to God, to Satan, and yourself, can you then turn to put right relationships with others.

If the first three things involve being told what to do, we are now told what *not* to do towards our brothers. The basic thing is stop talking about them negatively. Once again, the initiative has to be with us. Stop being critical of your brethren, whether behind their backs or to their faces, but even more usually the former. Stop slandering. An awful lot of slander goes on in Christian circles. It is never brought to court because it is not public. Slandering or criticising your brother or sister, you have set yourself up, put yourself in the place of judge. Furthermore, you are putting yourself in the place of a lawgiver. You are virtually telling him how to live. That is a double fault. Having made yourself the other's judge, you are now telling them the law that person should live by. You are thereby criticising the law of God, which is to love your brother, wash his feet, and serve him. You really are getting very big for your boots, getting a big head when you make yourself a judge of your brother, and you behave as if you are giving him the law to live by.

So James finishes the passage. There is only one judge and lawgiver, and you must never try to take his place. Everybody is answerable to him and to his law. Nobody is answerable to you and to your law. We are all answerable to God. He is able to do two things: to save people, and to destroy them. That is why he is the judge and why he is the lawgiver. By his law, people are saved or destroyed. That is the ultimate result of God's judgement. So really James is saying: just who do you think you are? There is only one lawgiver and judge of all mankind and especially of your brothers and sisters in Christ. He will be the judge, and he will decide in the last analysis who to save and who to destroy. You are not God!

So, to summarise: the cure for these quarrels and conflicts is, firstly, to take the initiative with God, the devil and yourself (that is what to *do*); and then, secondly, there is what *not* to do about your brothers – stop criticising them; stop speaking against them, and speaking as if you are the judge before whom they stand. They will stand before their judge and their lawgiver, and you are neither.

I quote again that lovely little poem:

JAMES

Once in a saintly passion
I cried in desperate grief:
"O Lord, my heart is black with guile,
of sinners I am chief."
Then stooped my guardian angel
and whispered from behind,
"Vanity, my little man,
you're nothing of the kind."

We sometimes need to take ourselves down a peg or two
when we are judging our brothers.

10
RICH AND POOR

Read James 4:13 – 5:6

A. IMMEDIATE FUTURE (4:13-17)
  1. Presumption – self-confidence (13-15)
       a. Proposed excursion (13)
       b. Precarious existence (14)
       c. Providential exposure (15)
  2. Pride – self-congratulation (16)
       a. Boasting is common
       b. Boasting is evil
       Note on sins of omission

B. ULTIMATE FUTURE (1-6)
  1. Testimony
       a. Your wealth – rotted
       b. Your workers - resentful
  2. Verdict
       a. Luxury – indulgence of self
       b. Cruelty – indifference to others

Again James has a real go at the rich. He has got it in for them, there is no doubt about it! I want you to notice he calls everybody "brothers" except the rich. The rich he simply calls "the rich". To them he says, "Now listen", a very brusque demand for attention. It is almost as if he fears that rich people will not listen carefully, so he appeals twice to them at the beginning of each of the two sections of this part of the letter: now listen, I've got something to say to you that you will not want to hear, that you do not like, but you ought to listen. The two "listens" refer to the immediate future and the ultimate future of these rich men. He is talking about their plans for the next year, the immediate future, and then he is going to look right ahead to a day when all their wealth will have gone. These are the two aspects he wants to challenge the rich brethren about.

Remember that James is writing to Messianic Jews in the Dispersion, and that their spread throughout the known world was for trading, for business. James three times has such a go at the rich brethren, who are his brothers, but he refuses to call them that because of the way they are behaving.

Let us look first at their immediate future, and if there is one thing that characterises it, it is self-confidence. Their plans stretched a year ahead. They were so confident that they would be healthy and able to do it that they simply said, "We will set off today or tomorrow, we'll go to such and such a city to do business, stay there a year and make money and then come back richer people." All this was said so confidently, as if nobody could interfere with their plans, as if they were in total charge of their own lives. That is something that James wants to comment on. It is a business maxim that if you do not expand you die, you have to be building the business up all the time or else it will go down. So they were virtually planning to extend their business in new cities and open up new branches of their trading. They would have staff whom they took with them and staff who stayed at home to look after the accounts. But they themselves made confident plans. James has to remind them that life is precarious; you cannot bank on the plans you have made.

The classic example of this was Alexander the Great. His ambition was to conquer the then known world. He got as far as Babylon and at the ripe old age of thirty-two contracted fever and died. This was the man with an army and he set off in great confidence. Everybody knew him as "Alexander the Great". James says: "What is your life? It is like a morning mist, like a vapour that appears and disappears." We need to remember that in all our plans we make for the future. Life is precarious, you can't bank on it, you can't be sure that it is going to happen.

I remember meeting a retired headmistress in the Cotswolds whose husband was a retired headmaster. They had saved up all their lives for their retirement and they bought a most lovely "chocolate box" cottage in the country, down a lane far from anywhere – real country life. They looked forward to spending many years together. Within two months he had died and she was left all alone in this country cottage. They had banked on a future that was not to be theirs. Mind you, she was a lovely Christian and she laid her problem before the Lord and said, "What can I do for you here in the middle of the country? Please give me someone to witness to." The very next day a young lady rode by on a horse – she lived on an estate down the road. The retired headmistress made friends with her and met her every day to talk to. The lady on the horse was Princess Anne. Many people noticed that she became a rather softer person and not so hard as she had been, and it was through this dear retired headmistress witnessing to her. Life is like that– it could go tomorrow, and we need to remember that, James is teaching.

Therefore he writes: "When you say, 'I'm going to such and such a city and I'm going to do business for a year and I'm going to get rich and come back,' you should say it a little differently. Say, 'If the Lord wills, I'm going to do that.'" That is a little way of making a testimony, a witness to your colleagues at work and to those who know you. Don't say, "I'm going to do this," say, "I'm hoping to do this." There is nothing here against making plans for the future. But there is everything against stating those plans to other people as if you are in charge of your own life, as if you can decide these things. If you say, "I'm going to go and make money," you just may be gone. In all this James is echoing his brother, Jesus, because Jesus said there was a man who said, "Let's expand the business, pull down our barns, build bigger barns," and Jesus said, "You fool! You idiot! Tonight your soul is required of you, and you're making plans as if you're here forever." Of course we have all got to admit this – we tend to think as if we are here forever. If we are not careful we forget.

We had an undertaker in our church in Guildford and he never once thought about his own death. He was handling dead bodies all the time as a job and he never once realised that he was going to die (this was before he came to the church). It took his little daughter, a girl of about eight, who said to him, "Daddy, where will you go when you die?" It was the first time he had ever thought about it, and he became a Christian and got a faith in the real future. I asked him to give his testimony in the church and he got up and said, "Nobody likes to shake hands with me when I tell them I'm an embalmer of dead bodies, and they put their hands back in their pockets." I remember that a kind of wave of negative reaction went through the congregation when he told us what his job was. But it took that little girl to get him to think about his own death.

In any group of people someone is going to be the next to die, and it may not be the oldest person. You cannot bank on life. But you can bank on the will of God. Therefore you need to say, "If God wills, I plan to do this." My father used to write that regularly in letters. He would write in brackets, "DV". That has gone out of use now, but it means "Deo volente" – God willing, especially if he committed himself to anything for the future. When you study your New Testament you find that most of the apostles had developed that kind of habit.

Now funnily enough, we are challenged in this by the Muslims. Their favourite saying is "Insha'Allah" – if Allah wills. They have overdone it and it has almost become a kind of fatalism. I remember being in an Arab village where a villager had been out fishing. He had come back with a good catch and laid all the fish out in the sand for the sun to dry it (their only way of preserving food). It came on to rain. It only rained three times a year at most in that part of Arabia, and then it really rained. I said to him, "Shall I help you gather your fish in before the rain ruins it all?" The man just said, "Insha'Allah" – and that was it. He stood there and watched all his fish rot in the rain. That is fatalism.

But I did hear more Muslims say, than I have heard Christians say "if God wills". That is worrying. What are your plans for the future? Do you say you will do something if God wills or have you just made the plans regardless? God's will is supreme and can override any plans we have made, so let us get into the habit of saying, "If it is his will", because nobody knows when God will overrule something.

In Ecclesiastes 3 (and I refer you to my book *Unlocking the Bible*) the message is this: God is sovereign; he decrees. God will decide whether you live or die this next week. He can overrule all your plans, and that is what James is really saying.

James turns now to his second aspect of this confidence, namely pride. Presumption is a form of pride and it certainly leads on to pride. Connected with a planned excursion for trading is an arrogance that can boast beforehand of what it will achieve and, afterwards, of what it has achieved.

Boasting is very common. Pride is the most common sin, and so boasting is the most common form of speech, especially boasting about your own achievements. As a poet said, years ago, "I am the captain of my soul; I am the master of my fate." Notice there that both lines begin with "I am". It is so easy to think of yourself as the "I am" who is in charge. Therefore you boast both before and after. Someone told me that the god of the United States is success. I believe it. It has even got into church circles – you hear claims to be a successful church. Often a public speaker from the States is introduced as, "He's the pastor with three thousand members," or twelve thousand members, or what have you, as if he is a "successful" pastor. If we are not careful we pick up that habit too. Our ambition is to be successful, and when we are we tend to boast: "I'm a successful person, I have succeeded in my goals."

Notice that boasting is evil. It is wrong, especially when it is about yourself, your family or your achievements. It is pride, and that is the deadliest sin of all, according to the Bible. James says that all such boasting is evil. He is not saying that all boasting is evil. There is a kind of boasting that is valid. The only boasting he is condemning as evil is the boasting about your own achievements, and that is so very easy. When we project our achievements onto our family we boast about the family too.

Boasting about achievements is never acceptable to God, but there is a boasting that is acceptable to God. Consider some verses from 2 Corinthians 10, and I want you to notice that in every verse the word "boast" comes and Paul is doing the boasting:

> We, however, will not boast beyond proper limits, but will
> confine our boasting to the field God has assigned for us,
> a field that reaches even to you. We're not going too far
> in our boasting, as would be the case if we had not come
> to you, for we did get as far as you with the gospel of
> Christ. Neither did we go beyond our limits by boasting
> of works done by others. Our hope is that, as your faith
> continues to grow, our area of activity among you will
> greatly expand so that we can preach the gospel in the
> regions beyond you, for we do not want to boast about
> work already done in another man's territory. But let him
> who boasts, boast in the Lord.

Did you notice how often Paul used the word "boast" in
that short passage? Five verses, and "boast" occurs in every
one of them. It is Paul the apostle, and that boasting that
Christians can do and should do regularly. Boast about what
the Lord is doing, our Lord and Saviour – boast about him.

I remember being at a cocktail party (which is not my
scene) in London and a businessman came up to me and
said, "And what's your business?"

I said, "I'm the pastor of a church."

He said, "What's it like belonging to a dying organisation?"

I replied, "I wouldn't know."

He said, "What do you mean? The church is dying
everywhere."

"Not everywhere, though maybe in this country. Every
minute I talk to you we have another 45 customers in the
church worldwide. Multiply that by sixty and that is what
is happening every hour. Multiply that by twenty-four and
that is what is happening every day. Multiply that by seven
and that is what is happening every week. If your business

was increasing like that, wouldn't you be boasting?" He had never thought of the church as growing that fast, but it is growing more quickly today than it has ever grown before, and we need to boast about that. Christ is building his church and he is doing it very successfully. Let us boast about that and let people know what he is doing, and that is what Paul says.

Verse 17 summarises this whole section in typical unconnected fashion and is a reminder of a very profound principle: that if you know a good thing to do and do not do it, that is sin – a sin of omission in God's sight. That is quite serious, is it not? It means you may never do any bad things, but you may not have done some good things that you could have done and that you knew you ought to have done, and both are sinful. So James reminds us all of that profound principle – you have been warned. If James were addressing us today, how would he apply this whole section? I think he would underline two things. First of all, making plans for the future. Whether it is for your retirement or for your new job, for your holidays, in fact, any dates you put in your diary you should add a mental "DV". I stopped taking dates for more than about six months ahead. I used to take them two or three years ahead, but now I have realised: how do they know what God is wanting to happen then? But it is usually people who have an anniversary and they tell me they need to book ahead to get any decent speaker. What a motivation! But I don't know if I will be here in six months or even tomorrow, so I have cut down on future commitments just as a matter of not presuming I am God.

I am sure that James would say making future plans without reference to God is a mistake for all of us. But what would he say to those who make money and make that their main objective in life? In Victorian days we were called a nation of shopkeepers. I would call us a nation of gamblers today because that is the new way to make money quickly and easily – ranging from the humble raffle ticket right up to the National Lottery, where you can earn millions without working at all. Unfortunately our government is feeding that and has encouraged people to get into the gambling habit.

Let us define gambling quite clearly so that we know what we are talking about. There must be three things happening together to make anything a gamble, whether on the stock exchange or anywhere else. First, you are gaining money without earning. That is, you are receiving money without giving any goods or services in exchange for it. By itself that is not gambling. It could simply be receiving a gift, receiving a legacy. The second thing that needs to be present is gaining at other people's loss, so that everything you benefit from comes out of somebody else's pocket. Even if they are willing to lose their stake, that makes no difference – you are still hoping to gain at their loss. But there is a third necessary element. That is that you are creating a risk that you did not face before. That is what distinguishes gambling from insurance. Insurance is against risks you already have. You are not creating the risk, you are insuring against it because it is a real risk for you. But when those three factors come together, it is gambling. I do believe that every Christian should have a very firm stand against all forms of gambling. You cannot be loving your neighbour and wanting him to lose so that you can gain – it is impossible. I think James would want to say something about that form of making money today. I think he would also want to say something about the credit society. We have all learned to get into debt through plastic money. You are not in debt unless you have not paid up when the money was due. A mortgage is not a debt until you get behind with payments.

Becoming a credit society has also helped the gambling instinct in us. At the same time, government is borrowing large sums annually to maintain our standard of living. They are borrowing it from the next generation, so our children and grandchildren are being forced to pay for our standard of living. There is an outcry when our standard of living is reduced, as it ought to be because we are in debt. Our nation is in debt, they are borrowing money to keep us going, to keep our National Health Service going, to keep our welfare system going.

So we live in this debt-ridden society in which it is so easy to get into debt ourselves. You get into debt when you want something you cannot afford – when you want a better house while mortgage interest is low, and then when the interest goes up you find you cannot afford the mortgage. That is how people get into debt, when they want more than they have, in other words, when they covet something they do not have. I think all these things James would speak of today, trying to apply his principles to where we are.

Let us now turn to the second subject. James now talks about their ultimate future to rich people who want to make money quickly and easily. Again he says: "Now listen...." He realises they will not want to listen, that he has to fight for their attention. He is going to describe their ultimate future now because that is how a Christian lives: we look ahead to that day of all days, which is coming to all of us, which involves the day of judgement. It involves the return of the Lord Jesus. It involves our accountability to God for how we have lived.

So James is posing the question: how will you feel then about what you are planning to do now? Take the long-term view. Imagine yourself in a future that is absolutely certain to come, and ask yourself how you feel now about what you are doing. We are the people of the future; we live in the future and we live for the future. We judge the present by the future, and that is a key perspective for Christian living.

So James is reminding them: one day you are going to be on trial for your life and God will decide then what you are worth. The real worth of a person is not what they are worth now, but what they will be worth then.

Of course, every trial has testimonies. Two testimonies at that trial are mentioned here: the testimony of our possessions, our wealth, and the testimony of our workers. What is the testimony going to be then (not now)? He actually mentions the word "testimony". The testimony of our wealth is that it has all rotted. No wealth will be of any help to anybody then, it will all have gone. He says "your clothes", and they would put their money into clothes. Your clothes will all be moth eaten then. In a graphic phrase James says: your silver and gold will have rusted. Gold and silver do not rust, so NIV has changed the word to "corroded". Gold and silver do not corrode, but he is stating a truth: your gold and silver will also have gone; you will be worth nothing. If your worth today is measured in your wealth, then at the trial of your worth you will be worth nothing, it will all have vanished.

Pursuing wealth, like pursuing pleasure, is a false aim in life which is going to leave you a pauper, penniless. You are a pauper on the day you die if that is what you have been worth to other people. It just teaches us to think ahead and not value a person for their possessions. If you are possessed by your possessions, then you will go as they do.

James says that they have hoarded wealth in the last days. What a foolish thing to do! It is like arranging deckchairs on the Titanic. A phrase that was used on the day of Pentecost is "last days". They began at Pentecost and we have been living ever since in the final era of history, the last days. What then is the point of hoarding wealth for yourself, building up a balance of far more than you actually need? How foolish, how idiotic, yet people are doing that.

What about the testimony of your workers? Here again James is scathing. The people who have helped you make your wealth, the people who have helped to mow your fields, the people who have worked for you. They did not benefit; you benefited from their labours. In fact, you even kept their wages back because of cashflow problems. These are serious indictments of rich people.

My wife and I are members of the National Trust and we find visiting old houses interesting. But at every one I go into I think: I know who paid for all this. I know scores of servants worked in the house or the garden to keep one family in comfort. I think of some of the great industrialists like Andrew Carnegie and John D. Rockefeller. Read their story, read where their wealth came from, and it so often came from a multitude of workers on minimum wages who kept the one family in wealth and enabled them to build their mansions. Our country is littered with that kind of mansion, and that is what it was built on. In that day the testimony of your workers could be just the wrong kind of testimony. They could be resentful of the way you treated them. It behoves every business person to be sure that the income is shared out with all who have contributed to that. I am not being political here but scriptural. If you are an employer, make sure that all your workers benefit from the wealth your business creates. It is very much on James's heart. If you do not, their cries will reach the Lord, and the Lord will remember everything that you have done to impoverish other people or make life difficult for them so that your life may be easy. I will leave you to think through the implications of this for our social life.

As mentioned earlier, once every fifty years the Jews had a Jubilee and everybody went back to their original income. The slaves who sold themselves were set free and if you had lost property it was restored to you in that year. It is as if God had said to his people: once every fifty years you all go back to level and you are free to build up again for fifty years. But he said he was doing this to prevent the rich from getting too rich and, therefore, the poor getting too poor. Read how communism began in Manchester, how Marx and Engels together were crying out against the few rich and the many poor in this land. They had something to shout about. Their solution was wrong, but their analysis was not bad. So on that day the testimony of your wealth will be against you, the testimony of your colleagues, workers and employees will be against you – what a testimony, and what a poor case.

So finally, this section finishes with the charges of the judge. The judge says "you" and that becomes the most prominent word in the last two verses. Here are the two charges: luxury and cruelty – luxury because you indulged yourself and cruelty because you were indifferent to other people in their need. Many businesspeople will face those two charges in the day when we all render our account. They are two terrible charges. God, who knows everything and has heard everything, will not make any mistakes in that day. If those two charges are able to be made against anyone, I would not want to be in their shoes, and I don't think you would either.

It is interesting that Jesus said all this in the parable of the Rich Man and Lazarus. A rich man lived in a rich house with gates at the bottom of the drive. Just outside the gates lay a beggar called Lazarus – the only person Jesus ever named in a parable, and Lazarus means "loved by God". Isn't that an interesting name? We are not given the name of the rich man. Lazarus was full of sores, open wounds, which the dogs came and licked. He would love to have had any food that fell from the table of the rich man, because the rich people used to clean their hands on bread rather than napkins. When the bread was dirty from their hands and their hands were clean, they would throw the bread under the table to be cleared away by a servant. This poor beggar, Lazarus, would have given anything to eat that dirty bread which the rich people threw away under the table.

No doubt they came in and out of those gates of the drive and saw the man lying there. It was not that the rich man was a bad person; he was not a criminal, he was not a cannibal, he had not done many bad things. In fact, it does not tell us that he did anything bad at all, yet he finishes up in hell and Lazarus finishes up with the angels – a very offensive parable which Jesus told, and he was talking to rich people. It was a case of self-indulgence on the one hand and indifference to others on the other. There are the same two charges of luxury and cruelty, and those two charges were enough to send a man to hell.

Living for self is behind all this section. It is a very short-term policy, because there will come a day when you feel totally differently about how you have lived. Therefore the appeal of James is to try to think that way now; keep reminding yourself of that future and you will find it changes your attitude to the present. How you feel about money now will change. How you feel about your possessions will change. It does not mean that you won't have any money and possessions, it just means you will feel differently, you will not become possessed by your possessions and you will not be storing up trouble for yourself in the future.

We are all in a position now to think of the ultimate future and not make so many plans for the immediate future with such self-confidence and self-congratulation.

11
PATIENCE AND PERSEVERANCE

Read James 5:7–12

A. PATIENCE – passive attitude (7-8)

    1. Example – from nature (7-8)

        a. Crop}

                Farmer waits

        b. Rain }

    2. Exhortation –

      impatience in speech (9)

        a. Don't grumble

        b. Judicial liability

B. PERSEVERANCE – positive action (10-12)

    1. Examples – from scripture (10-11)

        a. Prophets   b. Job

    2. Exhortation – integrity of speech (12)

        a. Don't swear

        b. Literal simplicity

James jumps around from one subject to another and you never know where he is going to next. But the two words I use as a title for this section are "Patience" and "Perseverance". Those words belong together as two sides of the same coin. If patience is an attitude, perseverance is an action. Patience is what you are, perseverance is what you do, so that one is a very passive word and the other is a very active word. How does this follow on from what James was just talking about, the rich and the judgement coming on them? He was telling them, you will remember, that Christians should live in the future. They should imagine themselves on the great day when they will give account and ask themselves how they will feel then.

There is one trouble with living in the future like that: the future is an awfully long time coming. Already in New Testament days there were people asking when the Lord was coming. All that James can tell us is to be patient; wait. He uses the example of the farmer. We know that this was a problem already in the days of the New Testament. At the end of the Gospel of John, Jesus is talking about the future of his followers and he tells Peter what kind of a death he is going to die. Peter accepts that and then says, "And what about John?" John adds in his Gospel that Jesus did not say John would survive until he came back, he only said, "If I want him to, what business is that of yours?" But a rumour started then that John would stay alive until Jesus returned.

Actually, he was the oldest of the twelve apostles. All the others died a violent death and John alone died of old age. There was a strong rumour in the early church that he would remain alive to see the Lord return. But Jesus did not promise that, and it was a rumour which should not have started. Here in James, written only thirty years after Jesus went back to heaven, already it is a problem with Christians that Jesus has not returned. If it is a problem for Christians after thirty years, what about us after two thousand? The simple fact is that Christians today find it increasingly difficult to believe that Jesus is coming back because it has been so long since he went away.

Consider 2 Peter. It is already clear when you read the last chapter that he has problems with those who asked: where is this coming he promised? Ever since our fathers died, everything goes on as it has been since the beginning of creation. So Peter himself was meeting with people who asked where this second coming was. Here we are, two thousand years later, and he still has not returned. It is understandable that the average church in this country rarely mentions the second coming of Christ. It is so far into the future apparently, so long since he was here, that some churches rarely mention that he is coming back, and you can understand that.

Jesus himself gave us fair warning. If we would only listen to Jesus we would not get caught up in feverish expectation. Of course every generation hopes it will be in their lifetime. I hope he will come back in my lifetime. If he does, it means nobody is going to measure me up for a wooden box. But it is getting a bit tight! I have not got much longer, so I am wondering if it will be in my lifetime. But Jesus himself warned us three times that he would be away for a long time. You find this in Matthew 25 where he spoke at least three parables about his return and how to be ready. The first was about a man he left in charge of his staff in his household. This man realised that he was a long time coming back and began to beat the servants. He began to take advantage of his position and cause the other servants to suffer. Jesus used a particular phrase in that parable – the master of the house was a *long* time away. Then he told the parable of the five foolish bridesmaids who ran out of oil for their lamps and the five wise ones who had enough oil to keep burning. Again, Jesus used the phrase: the bridegroom was "a *long* time coming". The third parable was about the use of talents – how the owner gave ten talents to one, five to another, and one to a third and then went away for "a *long* time". So three times when Jesus was giving parables about how to be ready for his return he emphasised that he would be a *long* time away, and he has been a *long* time away. That does not mean that he is not coming back. He did warn us.

The moral I want to draw is this: the real test as to whether you are ready for his return is the long time. If you believe he is coming back tomorrow, that is no test of your discipleship at all. That is panic. It is only if he does not come back for ten years, a hundred years, a thousand years, two thousand years, that your real faithfulness is tested. The question is: can you keep it up? Will you be a faithful and wise servant? Will you keep going even if it is not in your lifetime that he returns – not try to hurry it or to think it is tomorrow? If it is not even in my lifetime, how will I behave? Will I be faithful and keep up what he left me to do? Will I use the talents he gave me? Will I keep my lamp burning for a whole lifetime if he does not come back? That is the ultimate acid test of discipleship. Not if you think he is coming back tomorrow or next week or the next year, but if he is not coming back for another thousand years, how will you behave then? The real need is for two qualities of character: patience and perseverance. One is what we are, the other is what we do.

Let us look at the first quality of patience. It is a passive attitude. In fact, the Greek word used here means longsuffering (Greek *makrothumia*). How much can you put up with. That is patience. Notice that James relates the need for patience to the Lord's return. That is the biggest motive for patience.

Some people, reading James's letter, have questioned if he was a Christian at all or just a Jew writing to Jews. But there are unmistakable signs in the letter that he is a Christian. One comes early in chapter 2 where he says: "If you hold the faith of our Lord Jesus Christ and yet have favouritism of people, that is a contradiction." Notice "If you have faith in our Lord Jesus Christ" – no Jew who was not also a believer in Jesus would ever use those three words of him. They would admit Jesus was a man of history. But to call him "Lord" is to call him God and to call him "Christ" is to call him the Messiah of the Jews. But James does mention a profound Christian conviction here: that the Lord is coming; the Lord's return.

Only a Jewish believer would talk like that.

Some people want to hear you talk about the Lord's coming in such exciting ways that they get all worked up about it, but here is James: cool it, cool it; be patient, wait. Later he will use examples from scripture, but here he uses an example from nature – about a farmer, and that appeals to me. I kind of understand what he is saying. You can't rush nature. Every farmer, every gardener, knows that. That is why especially gardeners are some of the most patient people you meet. They seem to take life patiently. They know they can't hurry a crop. You put the seed in, you have to wait months for it to appear and become a crop. Anybody who deals with nature in any way has to learn patience, there is no other way. Now if your life is not closely related to nature, if you are just a travelling businessman then you do not have to be patient, you can become very impatient and try to hurry things up. Dealing with nature you cannot do that, so he uses a farmer as an example of patience.

In particular he mentions two features, first the crop. From sowing seed to getting the crop involves months of waiting. The other thing is rain. In the Holy Land particularly they are very dependent on rain. It only comes twice a year, in the autumn and the spring. They call them the early and the latter rains. The farmer has to wait for those rains because during the summer the Holy Land has six months of drought. There may be a little dew from the wind off snow-clad Mount Hermon, dropping down, and much of the wine comes from that dew during the summer in Israel. But the main crops of wheat and barley need the early rains in the autumn to germinate and the latter rains in the spring to swell the grain. Then it goes into a sunny, dry summer which ripens the grain. So a farmer has to wait for the rain and it is at the Feast of Tabernacles every year that the rain usually begins, and part of that feast is to pray for rain. In Jesus' day they would fill jars of water from the Pool of Siloam at the bottom of the hill, carry it up the hill into the temple, pour it out on the altar, and pray for rain. Every Feast of Tabernacles I have been to in Israel (I have been twenty times I think now) they pray for rain. Sometimes it has come during that feast, and a cloud from the west over the Mediterranean (no bigger than a man's hand, you can cover it with your fist) becomes a grey sky and then you get a downpour. So they get very excited—at last the rain is here, they can sow the crops and it will germinate. So that is the illustration used – a very telling example from farming. The farmer has to wait for his crop, he has to wait for the rains, you have to wait for the Lord's coming, and you will have to be equally patient because he will be a long time coming.

Now he follows the example with an exhortation, and the exhortation is not to allow impatience to colour your speech. If you are an impatient person it is inevitable that will express itself in grumbling and complaining. If you are impatient inside it will come out of your mouth.

So James adds to the example of patience the exhortation against impatient speech with others. If you are impatient for the Lord to return, that impatience will work out in your relationships with other people, and therefore you show an impatient nature. Since you cannot take it out on the Lord you take it out on people. That is a thing we are prone to do – grumbling against the Lord inside but grumbling against people outside, and the two are related. So don't grumble. He says you will be liable to judgement if you grumble.

Again, James is very close to his half-brother, Jesus, because Jesus said that for every idle or careless word we will be judged in the day of judgement. Did you realise this means that every word we have uttered has been recorded? When taking people through Ecclesiastes, we reached chapter 5, which warns you that God has recorded every word. Sitting in my congregation that evening was Charles Colson, the man who was jailed for colluding with President Nixon. He was jailed because they fiddled the tapes that Nixon had kept and cut out some of the words from the tape, and that was illegal. So Charles Colson listened to that sermon, and when I asked him to come and give his testimony after it, he just said, "You've already heard it, God had recorded all the words we've said in the White House and they were discovered."

Now James says a very interesting thing: the Judge is already at the door. When you hear statements in scripture like "the Lord's coming is near" the reference is more to space than to time. He is very near in space. Even though in time he has been away for two thousand years, he is only the other side of the door and could step in so easily at any moment; the Judge is at the door, as near as that. We need to remember that.

I can remember times when people did not have enough rent to pay the landlord and the man would come and knock at the door, and the family would not reply and would hide inside somewhere until the rent collector had gone. But they would understand the phrase "he's at the door". Jesus is just on the other side of the door and one day will step through and be seen back in history. The Lord's coming may not be in our lifetime, but the test is: are we ready?

He is not interested in what we are doing when he comes – it is a real mistake to think that. I think of one teenage girl I knew who haunted cemeteries and particularly she went to the grave of her parents all her spare time, spending time there because she wanted to be with them when the Lord came and they rose. She was not patient, she was neurotic. We are not to get neurotic about the Lord's return but to be patient and therefore we are to be persevering, keeping at it, keeping it up.

We turn now from the passive to the active side. It is interesting that Jesus' parables are all very active. The parables of the kingdom are looking after the household for the absent landlord; keeping your lamps burning during the hours the bridegroom stays away; using your talents and not burying them. It is very significant that it was the man who only had one talent who buried it. He was thinking by comparison: he's got ten, he's got five, why should I have only one? It is the person with fewer talents who tends to be the one to neglect using them. There is a lesson for you.

There is to be patience in the face of suffering – that is the first time he has mentioned suffering. But the New Testament says suffering is normal for Christians. "Whoever would live a godly life in Christ Jesus will suffer persecution," said Paul. You are bound to suffer. We live in a godless world, and if we live a godly life we will suffer for it. I was recently reading an analysis of the Middle East by a converted Arab believer who is so concerned that the whole Middle East is emptying of Christians because it is so tough for them. They are suffering badly. Women are being raped. Men are being beheaded for Christ as we sit here and grumble about trivia. Christians are suffering in many places at the moment. It is normal to suffer and the real test of perseverance comes when you suffer – because then can you keep it up? Can you go on doing it? Can you go on being faithful?

Habakkuk 2:4 became Martin Luther's golden text for the Reformation: "The just shall live by faith." But he misunderstood that text. Habakkuk was complaining that if God brought the Babylonians to Jerusalem no-one would survive because Babylonians had a scorched earth policy, not only killing everybody alive, but killing all the animals and killing all the trees too, chopping them down. Babylonians were such cruel people, that they would not leave any sign of anything living after they had been.

God had told Habakkuk, who had complained to God that he was doing nothing about the state of Jerusalem: "But I am doing something, I'm bringing the Babylonians." Habakkuk said, "You can't bring them, there will be nothing alive after they've been!" Then God said to him: "The righteous will survive by keeping faith." In other words, "I will protect those who live right by me if they keep that faith," and keeping faith in the Old Testament always means keeping faithful. It is used of a husband and wife who remain faithful to each other – a lovely word – "keeping faith" – Habakkuk, the righteous will survive by keeping faith, even when the Babylonians are here and everything looks dreadful.

That is why in the final chapter the prophet Habakkuk rejoices: "Though the fig tree doesn't blossom, and the vine produce no fruit, yet will I rejoice in God my Saviour." We read those words, "though the fig tree doesn't blossom", and we don't realise what Habakkuk meant. He meant if they kill every tree I will still rejoice in God my Saviour, because God has promised. Now unfortunately Habakkuk 2:4 was picked up by Martin Luther ("The just shall live by faith") and on it he based his justification by faith doctrine and it became the battle cry of the Reformation. But in fact he got the meaning wrong. God was promising that the righteous would survive the onslaught of the Babylonians by keeping faith in God. God promised that survival.

For perseverance, James now does not look to nature for the example, he looks to scripture. Of course when James wrote this epistle there was no New Testament. By "scripture" he meant the Old Testament. So as he has done before in this letter, he goes back into the Old Testament to produce examples of perseverance. Let us follow him in this. He was saying: look at the prophets – if you want examples of perseverance, look at any of them; they kept it up, some of them against frightful odds in the face of appalling suffering.

Think of the three big prophets. As we noted in our study of 1:19–27, Isaiah was a man of filthy speech, but he never noticed it because everybody around him used the same bad language, until he met the Lord. Then the Lord cleansed his lips with a live coal and his lips were scarred forever afterwards, and the Lord said, "Now you can speak pure words for me, who shall I send and who will go for us?" and Isaiah said, "Here am I, send me." But when you read what God said to him then, it is appalling. God said, "I'm sending you to this nation, they will not listen. They will hear, but not understand, lest they be healed and converted. You will not see a convert for your ministry. You've got to preach to unseeing eyes and unhearing ears." That is devastating for a preacher – that nobody listens, nobody pays attention, nobody notices it. A preacher would be tempted to give up very easily.

Poor Isaiah said, "How long do I have to do that?" God said, "Until the whole tree of Israel is cut down and only a stump remains, until only ten percent of my people are left, and that will take you a lifetime of preaching to achieve." What a call! Unfortunately, whenever Isaiah 6 is read in public people finish the reading "Here am I, send me", and they don't go on to read what God sent him to do. God gave him a hopeless task, and yet Isaiah kept at that task all his life. Eventually the king of Israel was so evil that he ordered him to be bound and pushed into a hollow tree trunk and then he ordered carpenters to saw the tree in half with Isaiah inside it. That is what happened to Isaiah, but he kept at it until he was cut in two. In Hebrews 11, "some were sawn asunder" is a reference to Isaiah. Do you know they have been trying to cut his book to bits ever since – into Proto-Isaiah, Deutero-Isaiah, Trito-Isaiah, so they have not only cut him to bits, they have cut his book to bits. But he persevered.

Let us take Jeremiah. Jeremiah was a young man and

God told him: "You won't live to old age, so don't marry. There's no point in you getting married, your wife will just be a widow." But Jeremiah, who thought they would never listen to a young man, persevered. Even when they tied him up and dropped him into a cistern, which was a kind of well with water in the bottom. They imprisoned him, but he kept at it. They threatened to exile him, he kept at it; he persevered.

Let's look at Ezekiel. He was an older man, but he was told: "You're going to be a widower, and you must not cry when I take your wife from you because I'm not crying, though Israel has been taken from me, and you must show Israel my feelings."

So here we have prophets who were given a personal calling to embody their message, and yet they kept at it. Ezekiel kept at it all his life. These are the examples we need to follow, and says James, "We consider them blessed because they persevered, now go and do the same."

Then James brings another example from scripture, a surprising one – Job. You would have thought he would use him as an example of patience since we still talk about "the patience of Job". The poor chap lost his family, his business, his health, everything. His wife said, "You might as well curse God now because he's not doing any good for you." What a temptation. But Job persisted. When he was sitting on the ash heap at the edge of town, at the rubbish dump, scraping his boils, his friends came to commiserate with him. They said that you can't suffer like this without sinning. But Job persisted in his faith that he lived right and that he didn't deserve this from God, and he was right. We know the whole story – which he never knew – that Satan had come to God and said, "God you know why people love you: because you do good for them." God said, "No, I have some people who love me for my own sake, not for what I do for them." Satan replied, "Now, come on. What about

Job? You've blessed him with a healthy business, a lovely family, good health, that's why he loves you." God said to Satan, "Look, I'll give you permission to take all those things from him and see if he still loves me." Job persisted in loving God, he persisted in believing the Lord, and those three friends tried their hardest to persuade him otherwise. He persisted in his righteousness.

It says in chapter 1, "I made a covenant with my eyes not to look on a young girl with lust." He goes through all the things that he does to be a good man, and he says, "I don't deserve this, you are wrong." When those three friends came and said, "You've done wrong. God wouldn't let this happen to you unless you'd done wrong," Job persisted and said, "I haven't. I know that my Redeemer lives and in my flesh I'll see God." James says he did. We know about how God changed the whole situation later and gave him a new family, a new business, new health – same old wife, but she had stopped saying "Curse God and die" and she had come around to her husband's point of view.

So the end of Job is beautiful. I love the book of Job, especially chapters 38–39, where God challenges Job. He never tells him why it happened; Job was left in the dark. We know, Job did not, and he had to trust the Lord without knowing why it all happened. But God said to him: where were you when I created the earth? Were you measuring what I made? The cure for depression is to meditate on the hippopotamus. Now I recommend that to you. When you are depressed and thinking everything is against you, meditate on the hippopotamus. What God meant was: do you know why I created the hippopotamus? Oh, you don't? You never will. Thinking about the hippopotamus gets you out of yourself, out of your troubles. Finally Job said, "I've spoken out of turn, God, I should never have grumbled in any way. You are a good God." He said all that before God restored him, and then God restored everything he had lost and more, and did it in his lifetime.

Why is that an example of perseverance? For the simple reason that God doesn't act quickly, though we want him to. Phillip Brooks, the great American preacher, said, "The trouble is I'm in a hurry and God isn't." So often we are impatient with God because we wish he would do things quicker and settle all accounts by next Tuesday. But God can wait. God is both patient and persevering. That is why we need to be, because we are meant to be in his image and reflect him. That is why James says now, "God is full of compassion and mercy."

The story of Job is to show you how full of compassion and mercy God is, but he did not appear to be for years. This is the problem: we want God to be immediately as he is. We want immediate compassion, immediate mercy. He is full of both, but he is a bit slow – he is slow to anger; he is also slow to show compassion and mercy because God's time scale is different from ours. A thousand years is one day to him; one day is a thousand years. It is relative time to God and it is not relative to us; we want things quickly, especially in today's culture. We are immediate people; we tend to want whatever we want instantly. God is very patient. He can wait centuries before keeping a promise, but he will keep it. That is the God we believe in, a God who will always keep his word ultimately. That is why the Bible is so full of fulfilled prophecy. I have never tired of pointing out that there are 735 separate predictions in the Bible which God made, and of these he has kept 596 so far. So 81% of all God's promises have been fulfilled now. Most of the rest are about the end of the world, so thank God he has not fulfilled them yet. There are a few things he has promised to happen before Jesus gets back – out of hundreds, fewer than twenty. But we must be patient and wait for those to be fulfilled because they must be before Jesus returns. To give you just one: Antichrist must come before Christ comes. Therefore, since he has not come yet, Christ has not come yet and we must look for the Antichrist first, the 666 man.

Notice that James is back to saying "my brothers", and occasionally he says "my dear brothers", but he always treats his readers as "brother" unless they are rich when he does not call them that. When he writes "My brothers..." it usually introduces a new subject. Sure enough, v. 12 is on a totally different subject. If you ask me what is the connection with what he has just been saying, I cannot give you the answer. It is as if he pours out pearls of wisdom but does not tell you what the thread is that ties them together. "My brothers, above all, above everything I have already told you, I want to make this one point clear, don't swear." After the example of patience he gave an exhortation: "Don't grumble." Now after the example of the prophets and Job of persistence under suffering, he says, "Don't swear." I don't know why he says that at this point, but we must take notice of it because he says: above everything, this is the most important thing I'm saying, don't swear.

What does he mean by that? It is not only using words in blasphemy or obscenity that we call "swearing" but something much more basic. He means anything we say to convince people we are telling the truth – that is what they meant by swearing in those days. Even just using the word "honestly". Have you ever said to somebody, "Honestly, this is the truth"? You should not even say that, it is swearing, bolstering your speech by an appeal, and you are appealing there to your own honesty. You should never need to say anything like that.

James is saying that our speech should be literally simple: your yes should be yes and your no should be no. Here again James is echoing his half-brother Jesus, who taught exactly the same thing: don't swear by heaven, by God, by anything else, just say yes when you mean yes and no when you mean no. Never say more than that. Always mean what you say and always say what you mean, and people will trust your speech. You don't need to say "Honestly"; you don't need to say "I'm telling the truth." Sooner or later the people who know you will know that you mean what you say.

How important this is to parents of little children – always to say what you mean and to mean what you say. If you threaten your child with punishment, then punish them. Don't let them realise that you aren't meaning what you say. So threats of any kind, appeals of any kind to truth, are unnecessary for the Christian; swear not by anything at all, let your "yes" be yes and your "no" no is James's most important exhortation. Strange choice, but there we are.

James is a letter of duty, not of doctrine, therefore there is very little doctrine in this letter. That is why Martin Luther did not like it much. But there are a lot of dos and don'ts, and that is not very exciting. I was trying to think of a title for the whole letter, and the one that seemed to appeal most to people was "Now Do It". I think that is my summary of it. But there are "don't"s as well as "do"s, so I suppose it should be called The "Do"s and "Don't"s. Here is a man who can mention the second coming of our Lord and tell us nothing but "Be patient and wait". That is so important.

12
SICKNESS AND SIN

Read James 5:13–20

5:13-20 SICKNESS AND SIN
Troubled? Pray
Cheerful? Sing
Sick? Call elders

A. SEVERE WEAKNESS (13-18)
    1. Anointing (14)
        a. Elders
        b. Oil
    2. Interceding (15-16)
        a. Confident faith
        b. Confessed sin
        c. Consistent righteousness
Encouraging example: Elijah (17-18)

B. SERIOUS WANDERING (19-20)
    1. Amble away (19a)
        a. From the truth – the way
        b. To error – his way
    2. Brought back (19b-20)
        a. Save his soul from death
        b. Hide a multitude of sins

There is a distinct change in the letter of James at this point. Until now he has been telling individuals how to do and not do the Christian life, and it has been addressed mainly to Jewish believers in Jesus, but also to Gentile believers like us. But here he is talking about the community, the church, and our responsibilities for each other. So there is quite a distinct change from the personal to the pastoral situation. A corporate notice has come in about our mutual care, our mutual concern, our mutual compassion as believers one for another.

James begins the passage with a machine gun, firing bullets: Any of you in trouble? This is what you should do. Any of you happy? This is what you should do. Any of you sick? This is what you should do. The emphasis is on what each of us in these situations should do about it. There is a Christian duty to do something about your moods. Take the first one: "Is any of you in trouble?" The word means vexed, afflicted, troubled. Have you got some troubles? Then you know what you should do. Pray about it, go to your heavenly Father; ask him about it.

"Is any of you happy?" The word is actually cheerful – in good spirits. Then you know what to do about it: sing! Use your voice all the time. Either pray when you are in trouble or sing when you are not. Which do you think we mostly neglect? I think most people pray when they are in trouble, but they neglect to sing praises when they are happy. I don't see why you should claim one of these and not all three. So if you are sick and you want to do something about it, then did you sing when you were well? Or did you just ignore that and do what you do when sick or when trouble comes?

It is the third point that he expands on. "Is anyone sick? Let him call the elders, let them anoint him with oil", and so on. He expands this last one into four verses, during which he mentions prayer seven times in all – in just a few verses.

It is prayer that heals the sick, not oil. I want to underline that because people can have a magical view of oil, which James does not have. He states specifically: let them anoint him with oil and the prayer will raise him up. The prayer will heal him, not the anointing. The anointing is part of it, but it is not the whole secret. There is nothing magical about the oil.

Let us look at it in detail. We are trying to tackle the question: is healing the sick a normal part of church life? Or if it is not, should it be? We can race through the centuries. Every Christian I know believes that Jesus healed the sick. It is an integral part of the gospel and you cannot get away from it. They brought the sick to Jesus in great numbers and he healed them all. All Christians believe that Jesus healed the sick and that he did so by the power of the Holy Spirit and as a sign of the kingdom. There is no question about that.

Secondly, most Christians I know believe that the apostles healed the sick and continued Jesus' work. They raised the dead – as Jesus raised Lazarus from the dead, so the apostle Peter raised Dorcas from the dead. So there clearly is a link between the Gospels and Acts. The apostles who had been sent out to heal the sick in the days of Jesus continued to do it after he ascended into heaven and left them. So there is no argument about that. But there is a big argument about this: were the healing miracles limited to the apostles, and when they died out did the healing ministry of the church cease? Many teach and believe that the miracles of healing belong to the apostolic age, to the apostles who had that power.

But here is James disagreeing with that profoundly. He is saying it is the job of the elders of the local church. He does not say it is the apostles who healed, and that therefore because there are no apostles of that kind today we cannot expect healing today. James is treating this as a normal part of local church life, and the elders as such being the channel of healing. Those who disagree with limitation to the apostles point out that the gift of healing is one of the gifts given by the Holy Spirit to the ordinary church members among other gifts such as tongues, interpretation, miracles and so on. There is the gift of healing, not for everybody but at least for some – there will always be some who have the gift of healing.

In church history, the first thing that happened is that generally healing miracles went into decline. One could argue that was because they got away from scripture and that their faith changed. Nevertheless, it is a fact that healing miracles largely ceased to be a normal part of local church life over the ages. One extraordinary development that took place, based on James 5, was the limiting of the anointing with oil to those who were dying – and not to get them better. It was called the Sacrament of Extreme Unction. If you have any Catholic knowledge you will know that that is still the practice of the Roman Catholic Church. When you are dying and you know it and there is no hope, send for the priest and he will anoint you with oil and give you extreme unction, and forgive you all your sins before you go. What an extraordinary perversion of James's teaching! James is teaching about healing of the sick to raise them up, not to comfort them while they are dying. So that is one development we can leave behind as totally contrary to scripture. Through the ages there were some exceptions.

There were some rare occasional healings, especially associated with saints. Indeed, any saint who is beatified and then canonised in the Roman Catholic Church had to prove their worth by bringing healing miracles to those who prayed to them. That is still the case. Cardinal Newman was the latest Englishman to be beatified. Before he can be canonised and called a saint and given a saint's day in the calendar, there will have to be two or three healing miracles of people who prayed to him even though he is dead. That is how the Catholics developed James 5, and you can see the difference straight away.

In the twentieth century there was a wide scale return to the healing ministry of the church, largely through the Pentecostal denomination and the charismatics in other denominations. Because healing is a gift of the Holy Spirit for the church there has been a widespread restoration of belief in healing the sick as a normal ministry of the church. Though it is often concentrated in healing evangelists today, people who go around the world evangelising but at the same time healing the sick, there are also special healing meetings held by some churches on a regular basis. Though I have to confess they have concentrated on what is called "inner healing" for the most part. While there have been some physical healings, the majority of claims for healing have been applied to the inner emotions rather than the outer bodily afflictions. So it is a mixed bag.

All churches today believe they should pray for the sick, but it usually stops there. Praying for the sick is quite a different thing from healing the sick. Most churches finish their intercessory section of worship by asking the congregation to pray in silence for any you know who are sick, and that's it. There is usually no record kept of who has been prayed for, and certainly no record reported to the congregation of the results of those prayers. But it has become a regular part of corporate intercession to pray for the sick members of the church.

So what is the truth of it all? I believe truth is in scripture and James 5 is crucial. I am going to dare to give you my testimony because it was through these verses in James 5 that I got filled with the Spirit. Many have already read my story, but let me repeat it briefly. There was one man in our church who was the self-appointed leader of the opposition, and I have discovered that God puts one such person in every church to keep the leaders humble. His name was James, and he was the bane of my life. I used to come home from church meetings so depressed, and say to my wife, "There's James again, opposing everything I want to do." She would say to me, "Look, all the other members are with you. It is only James who's opposing, so don't let him bother you so much." But he did. He was a clever man who worked in the patent office in London. There were two reasons why he opposed anything I suggested. One was that we had done it before and it didn't work and the other was that we had never done it before and shouldn't try. Between the two I got nowhere with him and he became my thorn in the flesh. Once a year I had relief from him because he used to develop in the early spring a kind of acute hay fever which filled his lungs with liquid. He was quite helpless and went to bed for weeks until he was able again. Of course that was a great relief to me because there would be no objections from James in any church meeting. So I rather welcomed that little break every spring that came for a few weeks. Well it happened as usual about the beginning of June one year. I thought: "I had better go and visit him – after all, he is a member." So I went to visit him and all the way there all I could hear was, "James 5, James 5, James 5." I thought, "Well, what's that all about? His name is James, but what's the five?" Then I remembered that James chapter 5 has "Is anyone sick? Let him call the elders and anoint him with oil and the Lord will raise him up." But I didn't want him raised up.

Anyway, I went to see him on a Sunday afternoon. The first thing he said to me was, "What do you think about James 5?" I said, "You mean the passage in the New Testament?" "Yes. Would you come and do that for me? I'm due to go to Switzerland by air on Thursday morning on business, and the doctors put me to bed for weeks." He lay there, grey and gasping for breath. "Would you come and anoint me?" I replied, "Well, James, I'll pray about it." That is the usual cop-out for pastors. I did pray about it and I said, "Lord, give me one good reason why I shouldn't do this, please." And the heavens were like brass.

On the Wednesday morning his wife rang me up and said, "Are you going to come and anoint Jimmy with oil?" I said, "Alright, we'll come tonight." I phoned around some of the other leaders of the church and said, "Would you join me? I am going to visit James tonight and anoint him with oil." I bought a big bottle of olive oil, and we set off. Now before we went I thought I had better pray about this. I went into our church building, and I remember kneeling in my own pulpit. Now have you ever tried to pray for someone you were glad is sick? It is not easy. I didn't really know how to pray for him. I recalled Acts, where they were filled with the Spirit and healed.

I had never known what it was to be filled with the Spirit, and certainly not to speak in other tongues. I had arranged to preach a whole series on the Holy Spirit, for my good as much as anybody's, and arranged to come to Acts 2 on Pentecost Sunday, which I thought was appropriate. But the nearer I got the more I was dreading this. So sure enough I had got to the Holy Spirit in John at the same moment. Anyway, as I was praying in the church building in my own pulpit I was suddenly praying for James with all my heart, only not in English. I don't know what the language was, it sounded like Chinese to me. But I found I was praying for him with all my heart for his healing.

I remember looking at my watch and thinking "I haven't been praying for an hour, have I?" But I had. Then I thought, "I wonder if I can do that again." So I started praying and something like Russian came out. I thought: "This is Acts 2. What's going to happen tonight when we anoint James with oil?" I got quite excited. So we went, the leaders of the church and my bottle of oil. There he was, lying helpless, flat on the bed. I said, "We've come to do James 5." We opened the Bible to James 5 and went through it like you go through a car service manual. It said, "Confess your sins to one another," so I told James I didn't like him. He said that was mutual. Then I took the bottle of oil and took the top off and poured it on his head. And guess what happened? Absolutely nothing. I stood up and looked at him gasping on the bed, and I ran out of the room. I got as far as the bedroom door and I just turned back and I said, "Do you still have your ticket for your flight tomorrow morning?" He said, "Of course." I said, "I'll run you to the airport," and then I ran.

I didn't sleep much that night. The next morning I didn't want to get in touch with him and I tried to prepare a sermon. The telephone rang. "Hello, this is James. Can you pick me up at ten thirty?" I said, "James! Are you alright?" which showed my lack of faith. He said, "Yes, I'm fine." I said, "Have you been to the doctor?" He said, "Yes, I can go to Switzerland." He said, "I've been to have my hair cut and the barber said, 'Excuse me, sir, but I'm afraid I'll have to give you a shampoo first. I've never seen such a head of oily hair.'" Half a bottle of olive oil goes a long way.

I said, "Jimmy, what happened?" He replied, "In the middle of the night it was as if two hands squeezed my lungs and I coughed up a bucket and a half of liquid. I'm breathing." Now three things happened. One, he never had it again, and he had had it all his life. Two, he and his wife got filled with the Spirit. His son is now the International Director of CLC, a Christian literature distribution organisation. The third thing was that he and I became best friends.

Now you can call this all of the devil if you like, but I didn't think the devil was in the business of reconciliation, and James was the first person I went to when the Lord told me to leave that place and move to Guildford, and because he was my best friend I told him. James 5 means a lot to me. Prayer was the main thing here, not the anointing with oil.

So here is James saying, "If any of you is sick, let him call the elders, and when they come let them anoint him with oil in the name of the Lord Jesus." That is to say this is not us doing it, it is Jesus. That is to do it not in our name, but his. "And the Lord will raise him up..." sounds almost too simple. It sounds almost too confident, doesn't it? I have known elders try it and fail.

So James goes on to say much more. This is the third time in the letter he has talked about prayer, and every time he has given us a reason why prayer does not work. Have you noticed that? The first time, in chapter 1, he said prayer will not work if you pray doubting. If you wonder whether it will happen or not, don't pray, it won't work. The man who is doubting is like a wave of the sea being tossed around. Then he talked about prayer a second time and said: the reason why your prayers are not being answered is you are praying with the wrong motive. You are praying for your own pleasure, your own safety, your own comfort, and that kind of prayer does not work.

Now here he is saying, about prayer for the sick, that the elders should not only anoint, they should intercede and pray for the person, and it is the prayer that is going to do the trick. But he also says there are conditions of prayer, and these apply as much to the elders as anyone. But notice that he has assumed two great facts in the situation. He assumed, that the sick person is a recognised member of a local fellowship and not a lone-ranger as a Christian, and secondly that there are recognised elders, mature men who have been chosen for their maturity and who see healing the sick as part of the elder's duty. There are plenty of elders who don't see that today. They see it only as leading the flock or superintending the programme. But, in fact, from James we know that when a man is called to be an elder he is called to a ministry of healing, of praying for the sick, and anointing them with oil.

Not only is the oil not magical, it is not medical. Olive oil has medical qualities, but only when in direct physical contact with the cause of the sickness. Therefore it usually has to be ingested in some way – swallowed, rubbed in or whatever. The man who fell among thieves had oil poured into his wounds, and that would have helped seal them off from infection. But this is different; this is anointing you with oil, which usually means pouring it on the head.

How can that change the situation? What would be the reason for using oil? I suppose the same reason that Jesus used spittle. Jesus would anoint a blind man's eyes with his spittle. It is giving a physical reassurance to the person that the Lord can deal with physical things. To be anointed with oil is a very physical thing. You know it has happened, you can feel it on you, and it is a reassurance that the Lord can deal with physical problems. It is to confirm the faith that they all have. It is a very expressive thing to do. It is saying we will meet the physical need with a physical assurance.

But it is not the anointing that heals. It is their prayer with the anointing that is healing. James gives the three conditions which elders must meet to be effective in that kind of prayer. The first is confident faith – they must be sure of their faith. They must not be trying it out to see if it will work. We are back to chapter 1 again: confident faith is not doubting; it believes that the Lord Jesus will heal. They are not saying "May he heal", they are saying "We believe he will heal." Therefore it should not be undertaken lightly, unless there is that gift of faith to match the situation.

The second condition is confessed sin. Now you notice the little word "if". *If* the man has sinned he will be forgiven. There is a wholeness here, a wholeness of healing. Sin can be the cause of sickness – not always, but it can be because it sets up tension with the conscience that can wear a person down. Therefore confession must be part of this *if* sin has been part of it, but only if. The confession must be mutual; the elders confessing to one another and confessing to the sick person, and the sick person confessing to the elders.

Do you remember the man let down through the roof to Jesus? The first thing Jesus said to the paralytic was, "Your sins are forgiven." He said, "Which is greater for you, to heal the sick or to forgive sins?" So that is the second thing – total healing must take place.

The third condition is consistent righteousness. The prayer of a righteous man is powerful and effective. Therefore, you look to elders to be righteous men, and then their prayer will be powerful and effective. Those three conditions are there.

What does the word "sick" mean here? Does it mean any touch of ill health? No. Does it mean that whenever you catch a cold you can send for the elders and get rid of the cold? No. Does it mean when you get flu that you call for the elders? No. I want to tell you what the word "sick" means here because that is an important part of the teaching. It does not mean any infection you have picked up or whatever. The word "sick" is not actually used in the Greek. It is used in the English by many translations, but they are translating a Greek word that means "weak". The actual translation should be: "Is any among you weak? Let him call for the elders."

Let us expand on that. It is a very strong word. It means literally to be infirm, or to be helpless, laid low. That is my translation: "Is any among you laid low?" It means to be exhausted, to be helpless, to be lying down and unable to get up. It is a serious word. It means to be out of action altogether. It means to be disabled. When you study the Lord's healing of the sick in the Gospels you find many hints that this was what was meant. They always brought the sick to him, which means they had to carry them. They laid the sick out in the street for him to heal. Again: laid them out.

It is very interesting that the two words used for sickness here are, first, sheer weakness, and second, exhaustion. That exhaustion may be through overwork or neglecting the laws of health or sinning. It could have many causes, but it means really to be laid out, to be out of action, to be lying down unable to get up and do what you usually did. It does not mean old age, by the way, either, because when you get older you get weaker and more infirm. But it is not a promise for old age pensioners. It is a promise for those who have literally been laid low and are therefore unable to serve the Lord as they normally did; those who are exhausted, those who are helpless and cannot help themselves.

I think that offers a perspective on all of this that is important. Just because you are unwell or what we call "sick" I don't think it means you should be adding burdens to the elders of your fellowship. But if you who are normally an active Christian have been laid low and are lying flat on your back, helpless, then you qualify, and you send for the elders and they come.

We have looked at the three qualifications for the elders that are needed for effective prayer. Saying that might have discouraged many people. I can think of some men who would say, "I'll never be an elder, I wouldn't want to be an elder if you've got to be like that." So by way of encouragement James refers to Elijah. He was a man of prayer, but he was a very ordinary man. He was a man just like us. Now very few people think of Elijah as just like us. I certainly do not, but I should. For one thing, he had no fear of 850 prophets of Baal and Astarte, two pagan gods. He was not afraid of 850 men, but he was afraid of one woman. A man just like us. "Hell hath no fury like a woman scorned" – or spurned.

He was a man who was depressed and a man who got

so depressed he said, "Lord, I'm the only one you've got left." The Lord said, "Wrong Elijah, I have seven thousand left." But he was a man who got so depressed he thought everything was hopeless. Yet James says "he prayed a prayer" – that is the literal translation. It doesn't say in the Greek that he "prayed earnestly". It just said he prayed a prayer, a bit of tautology but there it is. He prayed a prayer and he stopped rain on the Holy Land for three and a half years. He prayed again, and the rain came again. Here is a man whose simple prayer controlled the weather for three and a half years' drought.

It was the same period as the Great Tribulation in the book of Revelation. It seems to be a kind of period in which God tested people, but there it was. Be encouraged; Elijah was a man just like us and yet he could control the weather for three and a half years by prayer. So he does not leave them feeling, "Oh, I'll never be good enough to be an elder." He is saying: of course you can be, you are just an ordinary person like Elijah, but you have got an extraordinary God. The one thing you have got that he had is the God of Elijah. When you pray, you are praying to the God of Elijah and all it needs is a believing prayer.

As I have pointed out, you have to be a recognised member of a fellowship and that fellowship has to have recognised, mature elders. Alas, many churches do not even have that and there are many Christians who are not even that. So we must be careful how we apply scripture, not do it too easily.

The first half of this last study I labelled "Severe Weakness" because I think that can communicate the meaning of "sick". But now we have a spiritual problem among members: serious wandering. This is not about somebody who deliberately turns away from the faith but who drifts away from it. It is about someone who is not directly committing apostasy, but who you notice has just drifted away from things and therefore has got on to a wrong road. You may know somebody like this who was running well with the Lord and then somehow just drifted and wandered away. This is where James goes back to talking about "my brothers" – if one of you should wander from the truth and someone should bring him back, remember this, whoever turns a sinner away from his error will save him from death and cover over a multitude of sins.

So it is not a deliberate, intentional turning away, but it is a wandering away. That is not so serious from one point of view, but very serious from another. Notice at this time the people to deal with this are not the elders, but any brother. Any of you could accept the responsibility of getting them back onto the right track. James is accepting that it is going to happen, and we all know someone to whom it has happened, and he is saying that if you are a believer, if one of you could turn him back, then do so. You have a responsibility. He has wandered from the truth.

Now is that the truth of doctrine or duty? Is it the truth of belief or behaviour? The answer is that it is both. You cannot wander away from the truth of what we believe without your behaviour suffering. Essentially it is from the truth, and therefore your job is to get them back into the truth. Notice that the error he has fallen into is "his way". The main title for Christianity in the New Testament is "The Way", but if you go and follow your own way, that is error.

The word that is used of this person means deceit, deception, disillusion, seduction, falling into a false opinion probably influenced by others, but in some way getting away from the truth. That is the wrong way and error is sin. But the main emphasis here is on the one who brings him back. Not the elders, *but* if one of you can bring him back to the truth and therefore to right behaviour.... Literally: if one of you turns him around. He is heading in the wrong direction and therefore needs to be turned around.

If you do that for him you have done two amazing things. First of all, you have saved him from death. That is the biggest thing you could do for someone. But what kind of death have you saved him from? It is not physical death, though sin can lead to that. It's the "second death" that the Bible calls it – spiritual death. That occurs after physical death and it is the one more to be feared. If you can bring him back, you have saved him from the death of his soul, not the death of his body. You have saved his soul from death, and that is the worst death of all because that is to be cut off from God forever. Now let me say it straight away that this is one of those passages in scripture which makes it crystal clear that "once saved, always saved" is not true, that you can as a believer wander away to such a point that your soul dies.

The first epistle of John ends with almost the same words, that there is a way that leads to death – spiritual death – so that none of us is safe. Therefore if you bring such a brother back to the true way you have literally saved his soul from the worst kind of death that would cut him off from the Lord forever. This is one of eighty passages in the New Testament that warns us about losing our salvation and believers suffering the second death. For this is a believer that has gone away: "If one of you should wander...." This is a Christian who has gone away, and he has got on the wrong way by wandering away from the truth. Therefore he is in danger of losing his salvation and of dying the second death. For it is not physical death that we need to be afraid of, it is spiritual.

The second thing you have done for him is to hide many sins, or literally you have covered them, you have hidden them from view. You have brought him back from a way that would have been increasingly scandalous and a bad testimony to his faith, and you have covered all that, you have hidden such things. There was one interpretation of this last verse through the ages in which it meant you covered a lot of sins of your own. But I don't think the words really will bear that meaning. You have covered a lot of sins of his – and hidden from the view of men and God what might have been had he continued on the wrong way.

That is the end of the epistle. It is a surprising end. There is no greeting and there are no personal words, certainly no signature like Paul used to sign his letters – nothing. He just ends. He has said all he wants to say and he stops, and that is probably what I should do now. Stop when you have finished. That is good advice to preachers!

Books by David Pawson available from **www.davidpawsonbooks.com**

Unlocking the Bible
is also available in DVD format from **www.davidpawson.com**

CPSIA information can be obtained
at www.ICGtesting.com
Printed in the USA
LVHW040736151118
597217LV00018B/321

9 781909 886728